DROP DEAD DANGEROUS

THE LETHAL ATTRACTION OF ROAD TRIP KILLER, PAUL JOHN KNOWLES

RYAN GREEN

For Helen, Harvey, Frankie and Dougie

Disclaimer

This book is about real people committing real crimes. The story has been constructed by facts but some of the scenes, dialogue and characters have been fictionalised.

Polite Note to the Reader

This book is written in British English except where fidelity to other languages or accents are appropriate. Some words and phrases may differ from US English.

Copyright © Ryan Green 2022

All rights reserved

ISBN: 9798354136209

YOUR FREE BOOK IS WAITING

From bestselling author Ryan Green

There is a man who is officially classed as "**Britain's most dangerous prisoner**"

The man's name is Robert Maudsley, and his crimes earned him the nickname "**Hannibal the Cannibal**"

This free book is an exploration of his story...

★★★★★ *"Ryan brings the horrifying details to life. I can't wait to read more by this author!"*

Get a free copy of **Robert Maudsley: Hannibal the Cannibal** when you sign up to join my Reader's Group.

www.ryangreenbooks.com/free-book

CONTENTS

Quick Draw 7
The Golden Boy 16
Prisons of the Mind 20
Prisons of the Flesh 28
The Heart Uncaged 37
Running Wild 47
Unfortunate Events 56
Falling Dominos 68
The Road to Ruin 78
Killing Time 92
For the Record 109
Close Up 118
Want More? 128
Every Review Helps 129
About Ryan Green 130
More Books by Ryan Green 131
Free True Crime Audiobook 135

Quick Draw

The Georgia freeway was swallowed up beneath Paul's tyres, the endless stretch of black up ahead being gobbled down and turned into history behind him. He never looked back, never needed to, never wanted to. Forward was where the excitement was—forward, just about anything could happen. He could be anybody, do whatever he pleased. The things he left behind him in a cloud of dust could only hurt him, but what was up ahead was hedonistic joy, the likes of which he could never even conceive of.

Yet all those coming pleasures paled when compared to the joy of this moment. A car, the open road, freedom. Infinite freedom. No locked doors or barred windows. Nobody barking orders, telling him when he could breathe or when he could shit. All the walls had fallen away, and he was living how he was meant to. Cities had their place, houses too. He didn't pretend that he never needed them, but he only felt like himself out here in the places between. Out in the grand stretch of nowhere land, not a cloud in the sky to hide the blue, not a car in sight to slow his roll.

From here, he could drive from one coast to the other. Switching from road to road, town to town, state to state, all in the blink of an eye. The world was his oyster, and if that meant he had to stab a knife into it to shuck out the good stuff every so often, he was more than willing.

Since back in Macon, he'd been riding in this new car. Cars came and went almost as quick as a tank of gas. When he needed a new one, there were always plenty of options available for the taking. Should the owner still be around, he was certain that their insurance would take care of it. It wasn't like he was really hurting anybody. Not by borrowing a car. They got them back, eventually. Or they got a brand new one. He was like the Tooth Fairy, replacing the old and unwanted with something better. Nobody could be mad at the Tooth Fairy.

This car wasn't his idea of a good time, but it ran and he couldn't complain too much. It had a full tank of gas when he climbed inside, and he knew that he wasn't putting anybody out by borrowing it. The guy that owned it wasn't even going to use it anymore. It would have just sat there, waiting to be sold off at auction to whoever had enough cash to throw around. Paul never had a penny to his name, but he didn't need it when he sidestepped problems the way that he did. Sure, he had to switch cars a lot, but that was good for him. New experiences were the spice of life.

His life had been very spicy this year.

Rolling down the window, he let the last of the autumn heat wash over him. It was warmer than it should be for Georgia; he must have been heading south all this time. He'd been so zoned out he didn't even know if he'd crossed the state line. Looking out at the green blur down the sides of the road didn't tell him much. If he rolled on for long enough, he'd see a road sign, some word or name would jog his memory. It didn't really matter where he went. Not really. Anywhere was as good as anywhere else. So long as he had a car and the road, he'd be content.

If he were somebody else, he probably would have worked out where he was headed next, but he wasn't. He was himself, and he would go wherever the road happened to take him. There was no reason to make plans—they were just prisons that people built for themselves. Even when they were free, they'd put themselves in boxes, lock themselves in and throw away the key. Marriage and jobs and houses and all that jazz. He didn't want it. He didn't need it. Love wasn't real. Stability wasn't real. You'd get fired from the job. You'd get evicted from the house. All it took was somebody saying the wrong thing at the wrong moment, and it would all fall apart. Why would he want to spend his whole life with a cop in his head, telling him what he had to say and do to avoid breaking out? He didn't need any of that.

A road sign whipped by. White text on more of the endless green. In Florida now. Georgia not far behind. Either was good. Either had its opportunities.

Forget about that nine-to-five life in a box. Kissing the kids and paying the bills on time. This was all that he needed. Everywhere to go and nowhere to be. Empty of people, empty of chatter, just him and the roar of the engine. This was all that he wanted. All that he'd ever wanted. All that he'd ever fought for. His American Dream.

The glint of blue and red flashing lights in his rear-view mirror shattered that dream. The distant call of the siren ripped through the smooth rumble of the engine and set his teeth on edge.

The peaceful meditation of the road gave way to a spike of adrenaline. The car was hot, he'd committed crimes everywhere he went—he had every reason to be ready to fight or flee when he saw those lights flashing. Rational thought was not a common experience for Paul. Thinking back along a chain of events to where he'd been was like jamming his hand in a jar full of broken glass to look for the cookie at the bottom, but he did it all the same. Traced his way back to the last time he'd gotten laid, the last time he'd wrapped his hands around a throat and squeezed. Followed it along until it connected to the car he was driving.

They could track it. The licence plates would mark it as stolen. He was being chased down. They were finally on to him. With his face twisting into a rictus that might have been a grin, he pressed the accelerator to the floor. The engine's rumble turned into a roar, but Paul couldn't hear it over the pounding of his heart.

The chase was on.

The blur of green became a smear across the side windows; the windshield gobbled down road and reached for the horizon. Faster. Faster. The lights still flashed in the rear-view mirror but Paul had no time to look at them. He had to keep his eyes forward, anticipate the turns before they showed up—at this speed there couldn't be mistakes. No dithering, no daydreaming, no hesitation. Brain hardwired to the wheels. No room for fear, no room for guilt, just the road. It had always been his salvation, and he knew that it would be his salvation now. He had made his sacrifices—he had given everything he was to the road. Now it was time for it to pay him back. Justify his devotion. He wasn't a praying man, but if he had been, his god would have been a line of black tarmac stretching on through eternity. He would have been High Priest of the Highway.

Which would make the policeman still trying to keep pace the Devil—the one who wanted to take the sacrament of the road from him, who wanted to lock him away and throw away the car keys. These patrolmen never knew what they were riding on, they never knew the freedom they were trying to snatch from others, back and forth, back and forth along the same streets and avenues. Never exploring, never expanding—the same, always the same, day after day until they retired or died. As far as Paul was concerned, they were the very worst thing this world had to offer.

The Devil was on his heels, chasing him down.

So that was how he drove, wheels screaming beneath him as he turned off the main road, cutting cross country, blazing through dripping woods, out over open fields. The tyres of this old car were not up to the task, but he did not care how he ruined them. It was temporary—everything was temporary. From here he'd find a new car, a new prize, a new destination. Still, the damned lights were flashing. The distance was closing. The cops were getting nearer.

The Devil was looking over his shoulder.

He swerved at the last moment onto another crossroad, hammering the clutch, the brakes, the accelerator and away again. Dirt went flying when he mounted the verge, tail end brushing vegetation as it zig-zagged out of control. Then off he went again.

The cops had to slow around the corners; they had to drive like they meant to survive it. Paul didn't. He didn't need to. He had faith that the road would protect him.

He had faith that when he turned his wheel, the car would take him away to safety. He had faith that though the fuel counter flickered on empty, there was power enough beneath the hood to carry him to freedom.

Back out on the highway, he was able to really open her up again. Clutch up, no tentative pause, just hard on the accelerator and away. The cop car swung out behind him, all too soon, and Paul realised that he wasn't getting away. This old car had done him fine for cruising around, but it wasn't built for the chase like he was. The horsepower just wasn't there. The speed he needed to get free on open straights wasn't there. He was going to get caught, and he could either do it now or later. He'd never been one to flinch away from doing what he had to, he didn't get cold feet. If anything, that was the opposite of his problem. He'd always been too headstrong, diving into things too soon, too quick to act. It made folk that were slower uncomfortable. Once upon a time in some jail cell when a fight started up, he'd been the first to move. One of the other prisoners had seen it. They'd said it was something that happened to soldiers, to fighters, to the kids that had been knocked around the block one too many times. That little buffer of time between thought and action got eaten away by the things that they'd seen and experienced. It made them great in a crisis but a mess everywhere else. That's why his life was a series of leapfrogs from one crisis to the next.

Why he didn't feel alive if he wasn't on the verge of dying. As he sped down the highway, heading further and further south, with that cop car creeping closer in the mirror, he was more alive than he'd been in all the weeks of cruising around aimlessly. His blood was pumping.

There was no more point in running, but he still ran on, letting the cop close in, letting him feel like he'd earned it. Finally, when it seemed like the engine might burn right through and fall into the road, he put his foot to the brakes and pulled off onto the grassy verge.

It was so abrupt that the cop almost overshot him, slamming on his own brakes and twisting his wheel, skidding in a slow half circle across both lanes. Lights still flashing, siren still blaring.

Paul looked over at the policeman, no sign of fear showing on his face; he didn't fear the Devil. The devil was his adversary.

By contrast, the cop was flush with sweat, hands shaking as he fumbled with the clasp of his buckle and clambered out to stand, breathing hard, in the middle of the road.

This was the difference between Paul and the adversary. The adversary knew weakness; the adversary had no faith in the road.

He rolled down his window and, with what he considered his most disarming smile, met the Devil's mirrored stare and gazed at his own reflection. 'What seems to be the trouble, officer?'

This was the game. As if he hadn't just run him ragged across the state of Florida, as if it was all convivial and they were on the same side, and this was just a mix-up. Silly him, messing up some paperwork or going a little over the speed limit. What an easy mistake for anybody to make. The fact that the cop was quivering with barely suppressed adrenaline shakes and rage didn't matter. So long as he played his way through the script like he was meant to, there was a way out of this. There was always a way out.

There was no polite request for a licence and registration, just a barked demand that he get out of the car. Well - there wasn't much wiggle room there, no way to slide around the edges of it and find some way to turn it around. Maybe he should have pulled over before the chase, back on the highway. He shook that treacherous little voice out of his head as he climbed out and shut the door behind him with exaggerated care. He didn't want to be out on a main road where damn near anybody might come rolling by. He'd always done better in the back streets—unobserved.

The adversary was speaking, making more demands, shouting and screaming, losing his composure. That was good. That made him weak. Distracted. Paul could use that. He was shouting something now about turning around, putting his hands on the car, spreading his legs. Paul cocked his head to one side as though he couldn't hear right, like he didn't understand what was being said to him. He didn't really. His mind wasn't on words, it was on action, as it always had been.

It was an amazing thing to Paul that so much of what you could do in life, most people simply didn't. There were the little commonplace things, like driving along the middle of the road when there was nobody else around, but there were bigger things, too, like ignoring what somebody was saying to you. Taking things without asking. It was the biggest prison of all, that trap inside folks' heads that made them go along with what they thought they ought to be doing instead of doing whatever they pleased. It was as if there was an infinitely wide field, but everyone went trudging along the same muddy track in a neat queue behind one another instead of running free.

If you wanted something, you could take it. If you needed something, you could have it. Sometimes someone might complain afterwards, but all you had to do then was move along and find somewhere else to be. The road had been the answer to the question of consequences. The road had been the answer to all his troubles.

So, if he were to follow that path lay down for the dull and dreary to trudge along, then how the next few minutes were played out would be obvious. The cop would yell at him until he ran out of breath. He would read him his rights, arrest him, cram him rather unceremoniously into the backseat of his patrol car and shuttle him off to jail. He would stand trial, undoubtedly be convicted, and be locked away in some deep dark hole where the road was but a distant memory and his life would follow a new road that offered no turn-offs. Everyone knew that was what you were meant to do when the cops pulled you over. The cop knew that was what you were meant to do, too. He was running the same script he always had.

He thought his little badge and his little gun meant something. He thought that just because something had never happened before, it never could happen. All of them trapped in their prisons, following their scripts, understanding absolutely nothing. Sometimes Paul couldn't believe he was the only one who saw through the lie.

Nobody had ever strolled up to the cop all casual when he was telling them off. Nobody had ever ignored the shouted warnings as the cop went for his gun. Nobody had ever reached over, faster than the cop could, and snatched it out of its holster.

The adversary couldn't seem to comprehend what was happening. They were off script, they were in that vast unknown dangerous territory outside of the things that had happened to him before, and he just couldn't cope with it. His mind locked up, just like any normal person's would when it was confronted with a situation it was completely unprepared for. Any normal person, but not Paul. He was built differently. He was wired for life beyond the walls of society's jail. He was a free man, and that made him powerful. Dancing around the puppets on their strings. Stepping to the side of the rails as the train that was meant to crush him cruised on by.

The train that was Paul rolled right over the adversary. He took the cop back to his car and handcuffed him in the front seat, snagging the keys before he strolled on around to the driver's side. It was his car now. Unconnected to what he'd done back in

Georgia. Another tugging weight of history cut loose from his coattails.

He didn't believe in the power of the cops. He didn't follow their scripts and obey their strictures. But that didn't mean he couldn't use them. Anyone else out here that saw a cop car rolling up with their lights flashing would pull over like the obedient little sheep that they were. He'd have his pick of any car he saw.

It was time to take a ride, and the road would provide.

The Golden Boy

Paul John Knowles was born in Orlando, Florida, on April 25, 1946. Later in life, he would describe being born as the worst mistake he ever made.

It is difficult to say whether he would have developed criminal tendencies on his own, or whether they were a symptom of the conditions in which he was raised, but from an early age little Paul was always getting into trouble. His parents had produced a large family, there were five children and the two parents dispersed across the three rooms of their apartment. This in itself would not necessarily drive anyone down the path of criminality—there were a great many people in Orlando who lived in similar circumstances without ever resorting to the kind of behaviour that characterised Paul's early life. The defining factor in the family seemed to be a lack of care. Paul would describe it exactly that way: not a lack of love—because he remained convinced that his parents loved him until his dying day—but a lack of care. As though there was some block between loving their children and showing that love in any way. None of them were kept clean or fed or given any of the vital attention that would have helped to shape them into responsible adults. Their parents simply lost interest in them after they were out of diapers, and even earlier when the oldest kids started being capable of changing the youngest.

As a result, there was little to no moral guidance for the children beyond what they could pick up on the street, and that sort of morality focused less on high-minded ideals and more on extracting as much from others as possible before getting caught.

School attendance for any of the Knowles children had to be enforced by the truant officer, and without outside intervention, it is likely that not one of them would have spent a single day in the schoolhouse.

While this lack of care was all that Paul ever described of his early life, it becomes apparent from the recorded testimony of his brother, Clifton, that the situation was considerably more dire than that. Paul had a tendency to get into fights when he was forced to attend school. He won the majority of them, thanks in no small part to a great deal of experience with violence.

Much of that experience was gained from being on the receiving end of unusually harsh discipline from his father, who despite putting no effort into raising the boy, was always ready to punish him for any transgressions. By all accounts, the children all suffered brutality at the hands of their father, but Paul, in particular, seemed to be a favoured focus for his ire.

Perhaps it was because of the entirely casual way that the boy stole to feed himself and his siblings, perhaps it was simply the streak of defiance that burned in him even then. He would not tolerate being told what to do by anyone— not teachers, not the law, and most certainly not the man that he believed loved him despite all evidence to the contrary.

The two of them butted heads almost daily, with Paul always coming off the worse for the encounters, yet he still could not bring himself to back down. Even knowing he would leave with bruises and belt marks and the odd broken bone, he would not roll over and submit to his father's authority.

In modern times, all of the children would have been removed from the Knowles household and placed into care, but the support structures that have developed more recently simply did not exist in the 1940s and 50s. It was a parent's responsibility to care for their children, and if they chose to neglect that responsibility, the state felt no compunction to intervene.

After he was picked up by the police for stealing another child's bicycle and was delivered back to the family home with a fine, his father decided that he had reached his limit with the boy. Everything prior to this point had been a non-issue, but the moment that Paul's rebellion began costing him his precious drinking money, he had crossed a line.

At this point, he disowned his son and put Paul into the state's loving care, stating plainly that he had no intention of raising a criminal. As if he had done any raising up until that point.

From the first group home, it became apparent that Paul was going to be a problem for his caretakers. Even though he now had a source of food and a bed of his own to sleep in, his habits had been thoroughly ingrained, and attempts at enforcing the sort of firm-handed discipline everyone believed would be the best thing for him were stonewalled. He would come 'home' whenever it pleased him, ignoring the curfew and the rules that stated nobody would be allowed back into the home after the stated time. Rules only worked if they could not be circumvented, and by this point Paul had already learned the basics of house-breaking. Simple locks posed no difficulty for him, which meant that any attempt at stopping him from coming in had to be physically enforced by one of the staff.

Confrontation of that sort was fundamentally damaging to any trust that they might have been building with the boy, and in truth, he barely seemed to care if he didn't get back in, simply going off into the woods to sleep if he wasn't able to gain entry to a bed. It was as though he felt that there was no real difference between the two options. He had become so desensitised that he genuinely didn't appreciate any difference between a bed and the floor.

It was not as though there had never been a troubled child in the care of the orphanages he was bounced between, but usually, some semblance of order could be maintained despite them. This was not the case with Paul. He fought with other residents and staff as though they were his natural enemies. Violence was so normal to him that it didn't occur to him that there should be a day without it. Inch by inch, he lost what little sympathy the staff had for him as a child that had been deliberately abandoned and gained the reputation as a troublemaker, even here among troublemakers.

Normal disciplinary measures were attempted but to no effect. He had nothing to lose, and pain only incensed him and made him fight back harder. It seemed that none of the usual solutions were going to be sufficient. As a result, he was transferred one final time to the Arthur G. Dozier School for Boys, known at the time as Florida Industrial State School for Boys, near the town of Marianna in the panhandle.

Corporal punishment was to be expected in the orphanages of the time. Capital punishment was not.

Prisons of the Mind

Dozier was the final resting place for many of the worst youth offenders in Florida: Those who had committed serious crimes while being too young to face trial as an adult. Those who had pushed back against any form of discipline to the point that parents and teachers despaired. Those who were caught smoking in school. These were the hardened youths in need of reform who were sent to Dozier. They ranged from ten to thirteen years old.

The majority of the students were stowed away in individual unlocked cottages. There were also two blocks of concrete prison cells, though only the worst of the worst were supposed to be confined in this way. The campus was not fenced in. Control was maintained by the staff alone. At the time Paul was there, the school was still segregated, explaining the requirement for two sleeping blocks. A dining hall was also constructed during his time there, using the labour of the students.

None of these were the site's most defining feature. The feature which loomed large in the minds and nightmares of the students was the two-story building at the centre of the campus. 'The White House' was an eleven-room detention building meant for temporary isolation of particularly troublesome students. In practice, it was a torture chamber. Those boys that were placed into solitary confinement in the White House were often hogtied and left lying face down on the concrete floor for days at a time. Beatings were regularly applied, not only as a matter of discipline, but also because the staff seemed to believe that it would somehow improve the boy's morality to have their flesh flagellated. Whippings, canings, striking with fists. All were perfectly normal parts of the day in Dozier outside of the White House. Inside of it, things got so much worse.

Prior to Paul's arrival, the Boot Hill Cemetery had already been constructed on the north side of campus, but during his stay, it gained several new residents. The school had been investigated multiple times since its original inception because of the multiple deaths that residents had suffered and the number of injuries that had been reported. So, somewhat inevitably, the school stopped reporting them.

Few of the students who left Dozier ever spoke about their experiences there, and even if they had, they were considered to be beneath contempt by most of society. They were, after all, criminals and degenerates who had a vested interest in shutting down those few places that might curb their wicked behaviour. Yet despite attempts at whistleblowing being either ignored, swept under the rug, or downright denied, some slipped through the cracks and made their way into official records. The hogtied children were just the tip of the proverbial iceberg. A wide variety of assaults and torments were used against the students in the White House, where punishments too easily crossed the line from discipline to torture, and in many instances ventured into the territory of grievous bodily harm and rape.

When the school was finally shut down in 2011, the University of South Florida's forensics department were able to find over fifty bodies on campus, most of which were not buried in the graveyard. Making this even more concerning is the fact that over one hundred deaths had been reported by the facility itself although the majority of the records regarding those deaths were incomplete or had details deliberately obscured. The actual death toll of this reformatory cannot be calculated due to the lack of bodies and information, but informally, among the students during the period when Paul was confined, the expected 'dropout' rate was around 30%.

So into this world of rigid control, extreme violence, and sadistic rape came Paul Knowles, the boy who could not be made to obey anyone or submit to any authority. Predictably, he butted heads with the staff within minutes of arrival and never even got to see his cottage for the first three weeks. Instead, he spent his time within a cell of the White House where he learned that what he had suffered at his father's hands for all of those years could be interpreted as love in comparison to what these sadistic strangers wanted to do to him.

It was that realisation that seemed to shake him more than the acts of cruelty themselves—that he was being hurt not because they thought it would make him better, as he'd always been told, but because they were enjoying hurting him. Even the ones that didn't rape or grope his bound form or treat him like a chew toy were still getting pleasure from watching what the others did. And when their turn came to strike him, they did not hesitate.

The average stay for a resident of Dozier was six months. After six months, even the most hardened criminals were broken and compliant, willing to do whatever it took to get out of there and never look back. Paul was there for almost three years, suffering the worst that they had to offer and coming back for more.

In the course of his three years, a full third of the other residents of Dozier went missing, or they died in an official capacity, to be laid to rest in the graveyard. He had no meaningful ties to his peers but every day, as they dropped like flies, it weighed on him. He felt no pangs of loss, but the dull dread of inevitability. He had outlasted so many of them, but eventually, his luck was going to run out. They would choke him too long, or beat him too hard, or his heart would give out after another week of his own bound weight pushing it down against the concrete. Death hung over him every moment of every day as he did his chores under the guards' watchful eye, waiting for them to decide if today he was the one who should suffer—that the minor infractions that he had unknowingly committed were the worst of the day, and that it was he who should be sent to the White House to pay for their communal sins.

He came close to death many times in his years there, but for some reason, the line was never actually crossed. He did not die though dozens of others who endured the same treatment did. It wasn't because he was tougher than them, or healthier than them, or anything else. It was luck. Luck kept him alive. Any belief that he might have been clinging to that there was any order or logic to the universe was sanded away, day by day, until he was left with the cold reality that nothing made any sense, nothing mattered, and life was whatever you could grab hold of and enjoy for a moment.

Then it was over. One day, just like any other, he was pulled out of the usual chain gang and summoned to the gates, issued a set of clothes, and pushed into a car to be ferried back to civilisation. Once he arrived, he was ordered out of the vehicle, and with the obedience of a beaten dog, he climbed out to stand by the roadside, waiting for further instructions.

None were forthcoming.

The car pulled away and he was left there, rudderless and exhausted, with no idea as to what he was meant to be doing or where he was meant to be going. For some time, he simply stood there as the regular human beings that populated the world strolled on by and paid him no notice, until finally he started to walk. Each step, he was waiting for a shout. For a guard to come hustling up and hit him for leaving where he'd been left. He flinched each time a car passed by. But slowly he realised what was going on. He was free. His eighteenth birthday had been the day before, though he didn't know it. He was no longer a ward of the state, and the very instant that the taxpayers stopped funding his confinement and upkeep, he had been expelled from the school.

At the end of the street, he was confronted with three options, to carry on across the road, to turn left, to turn right. There was nobody there to tell him which way to go or what he had to do. He was free. It was overwhelming. All of that freedom after having none at all. All the choices of where to go next and what to do. He'd need to eat at some point; he'd need money. Maybe rent a room somewhere so he could lay down and sleep that night. That would require money, too. He patted his pockets and found them empty.

That was alright, his skills hadn't faded through the long years. There had been nothing else to replace them, just the white static of day after day. And the pain, of course. The pain, burning away any last shreds of decency and decorum that his father had tried to instil in him. It was then that he realised just how good his life had been when his father was controlling his life, that while he'd shown no overt kindness, the man had at least been trying to instil some sort of direction in him. Maybe that was love?

The things he did in those coming days would have made his father furious, but the fact of the matter was that he needed to survive, and if that meant breaking into people's houses while they were out at work and making off with their belongings, then that was exactly what he was going to do.

All things considered, he had a pretty good run of it. He didn't hurt anybody, just made off with their things, and when he finally decided he'd gotten everything that he was going to get from the town and it was time to move on, he stole a car.

It wasn't his first time driving. He'd learned back when he was still a child, but it was his first time out on the open road with the new mind that his years of torment had granted him. It was like that first moment when he'd been dropped by the roadside, writ large. Everywhere in the world was now in his reach, anywhere and anything that he wanted. For someone who'd suffered in confinement for so long, it was practically a religious experience. Bliss. He didn't pick a direction that first time, he just put the pedal to the floor and went. Letting the road guide him, turning when he felt like it, but only rarely, preferring the growl of the engine vibrating up through his legs to the twists and turns of the backroads. He drove and he drove until, in the middle of the night when he noticed his fuel gauge was starting to dip towards empty, he caught sight of a glimmer of lights up ahead. A new town, new opportunities. A new crossroad.

Money became an issue sooner rather than later, and he had to abandon the first stolen car in favour of another when the gas tank ran dry. He was inconspicuous enough that he could pass unseen through most of the towns he visited, blending into the background, committing petty thefts as he went. Picking pockets, pilfering luxury goods and selling them along in pawn shops. Just generally living the low life that he'd set himself up for.

It went well for him. He had always been talented enough, but confinement for years with the worst of the worst had honed his instincts and skills to the point that he likely could have gone on drifting like that forever. Taking what came in his way and looking for no more. As close to leaving no footprints in the world as anyone had ever lived.

After the horrors of Dozier, maybe that was all he wanted. Freedom and peace, doing what he'd always known best, but not really hurting anyone, except in the pocket.

Yet as the shock faded, Paul began to long for more. More than just the bare bones to keep him alive and his wheels turning. He wanted to walk into a bar and buy a beer without having to worry about paying in pennies.

Sometimes he even wanted to rent a room. He'd discovered the joy of women during this period, and being able to offer up a place to lay down made him a far more tempting prospect than back alleys or backseats. Even with those limitations, he did far better than he had any right to. Charisma hadn't been beaten out of him, nor had the good looks that he'd grown into and that had garnered him so much unwanted attention in Dozier.

So he scaled up from the petty thefts that kept him moving to more substantial crimes. Relying more on luck than good sense, he began to burglarise private homes instead of merely shoplifting and purse snatching. It was pure luck that allowed him to avoid encountering any residents while smashing in windows; it was pure luck that allowed him to meander leisurely to the next town before the local police realised that there had been a spate of related burglaries rather than simply one or two isolated incidents. It would be mere days after the fact when they'd find the stolen goods in the local pawn shops, all together, and realise there had likely been a single perpetrator. Despite that, they were no closer to knowing who was actually committing all those crimes. Paul was always long gone by the time they went looking. He was giving his life to the road, and the road was protecting him. This was the beginning of his mounting faith in it—a faith bolstered by the woeful lack of communication between police departments of small-town America. Just a few phone calls could have had cars waiting in the upscale residential neighbourhoods that Paul liked to hit in the next town along the freeway, but nobody ever made the connection, and nobody ever made the calls.

So, he abruptly went from being flat broke as he had always been, to having a seemingly endless supply of more cash than he knew what to do with. He had no bills to pay, no rent to stump up. All the costs of regular living passed him by, so every penny he could reap from his crimes was a treat. He could afford to spend the night in a nice hotel room whenever he wished. Ate the best food, drank as he pleased, smoked non-stop, and even bought himself some nicer clothes and a little case to tote them around in. Between his good looks and his attitude, the women that he wooed thought that he was some sort of rock star, and he did nothing to disabuse them of that notion until he'd gotten what he wanted and was on his way out of town.

The fear that had haunted him since he'd been freed from Dozier faded, day by day, becoming little more than a distant memory. A tingle on the back of his neck, and a nightmare that snapped him awake in the dead of night when he thought he heard the guards' shuffling footsteps outside his door.

He did not think about the things that they had done to him, because so long as he didn't think about them, they had never happened. Even when he'd talked some girl into bed and she was lying there, helpless and naked, just the way that he had been, he didn't think about it. Even when his hands pressed into their flesh and he drew out moans somewhere between joy and pain, he did not think about it. Thinking about those things made them real, and if they were real then he could take no joy in his life, he could take no pleasure in doing to these women what had been done to him. It would have been a downward spiral into madness and Paul was not going to go mad, he wasn't going to die, he was going to survive, no matter what it took or what it cost. Even if he had to amputate whole parts of his memory so that he could keep on moving forward, he would do it without flinching. Life mattered more than the places he'd been and the things that he'd done. The future was hazy and the past was a nightmare, but the present, when he had everything anybody could ever want—the lifestyle of a celebrity, the girls, the drink, the open road—that was something worth holding on to. The freedom of the road and the savage joy of successfully snaring some random girl, the prettiest in town, in front of all the scowling locals who knew she should be settled down with one of them—that was worth forgetting for.

He made it. He made it for much longer than he had any right to. He was almost nineteen years old in 1965 when he was cruising down the highway and police lights started shining in his rear-view mirror.

RYAN GREEN

Prisons of the Flesh

All at once, history leapt to catch up to him. All the petty crimes and burglaries, and the times he'd just snubbed the cops when they demanded respect. Which one of the many crimes was he being chased for? For how many years was he going to be sent back to some hellish torture chamber for having the temerity to live his life free of constraint? He stamped on the gas and fled.

As it turned out, the kind of old banger that he'd managed to steal unattended outside a bar at night was not up to the rigours of a high-speed chase. The speed he'd been going before was already close to the fastest it could go, so he'd barely made it a few miles before the cop was right on his bumper. He pulled up at the roadside like he was a good boy and let the policeman swagger up to the door and drag him out, shouting in his face all the way about the speed that he was going. If he'd thought Paul could be shocked into inaction by a raised voice, then he was in for a surprise. He'd spent every moment of his life being yelled at by some authority or another. It didn't faze him anymore.

This was the first time that he had truly faced a moment of stress or crisis since he'd been set loose from imprisonment, and he found that the old paralyzing fear that should have held him was simply absent. He had suffered too much for it. All that was normal inside his mind had been burned away. So while the cop yelled and remonstrated with him about his traffic violation, he watched, almost as though it were from a distance, as his hand reached out, took hold of the pistol handle on the man's belt, and drew it out.

He had never used a gun before, but back in his wild days of youth, he'd frequently snuck into the movie theatre. He'd seen how the cowboys brandished them. So that's what he did now, pressing the barrel up beneath the abruptly silent policeman's chin. 'Get in the car.'

They drove in silence for a distance, the thrum of the engine far quieter than the frantic machinery working behind Paul's eyes as he tried to work out his next move. Going with the flow had gotten him this far, but now a decision would have to be made. In a way, he let the road guide him once more, flying along, away from the abandoned cop car. If they hit a town soon, he'd disgorge his passenger and be on his merry way. If they didn't, he still had the gun sitting in his lap.

He wasn't a killer yet. He didn't have the drive to do it. He didn't have the anger or the blind hate to want to snuff somebody out just for crossing his path. He was praying for a town to come along, for him to be able to leave the cop in his dust and go on riding without a backwards glance. All he wanted was to be left alone. Why couldn't they just leave him alone? He wasn't doing anybody any harm. If anything, he was bringing a spark of joy to the lives of those he met. There was no good reason to punish him except to grind everybody down and force them to follow the same pointless rules that bound everybody else. They hated to see a man live free. That was all there was to it. And he wasn't going to let them take his freedom. Not now he had a taste for it. Not ever again. Not while he still drew breath. His hand drifted down to the pistol as the cop stared at the side of his head. He'd been talking the whole time, trying to calm Paul down, trying to make him see sense, trying to explain that there was no way for this to play out which didn't end with Paul behind bars. There was a wheedling tone towards the end. If he let the cop go without hurting him, things would go a lot easier on him when it came time to stand up in court. It had been spur-of-the-moment youthful foolishness. It could be forgiven, just like the speeding. There was no need for this to go to the end of the road. There was no need for this to become a tragedy, or for anybody to be punished like it was one.

Paul still hadn't made up his mind when another police car came bombing down the road towards them and swerved into his path. The cop had radioed in before making the traffic stop, like the good diligent officer of the law that he was. The other policemen knew where he was. They knew what he was doing. He wasn't alone in the world like Paul; he had a small army at his back.

He slammed on the brakes instead of trying to get clever, swerving around. Stopping was the only thing he could do.

Short of shooting his way out, there was no way for Paul to go but down. So he tossed the pistol back to the cop he'd taken it from and put his hands up, just like the cowboys in those Westerns he'd seen when the law caught up to them and they didn't want to be shot to bits. It may have been the first smart decision he'd ever made. Neither his kidnapping victim nor any of the other police had a clue what to do with him. Nothing like this had ever happened before, and if they were being honest, the idea that it could happen scared the hell out of them. If one person could interrupt a traffic stop by snatching a gun from the arresting officer, then everyone could. Just the knowledge that such a thing was possible would make their jobs infinitely more dangerous.

To make matters worse, the man that they forced onto the ground and cuffed did not look like some hardened criminal psychopath. He just looked like somebody's teenage son. He could have been anybody, and after his earlier actions, none of them could understand why now all the fight seemed to have gone out of him.

After his prompt arrest, he wasn't charged with his traffic violation at all. Not when they had a kidnapping charge to pin on him. While normally a media circus was stoked up whenever a crime was committed against a member of the force, if only to show that such a thing was completely unacceptable and would be punished to the fullest extent of the law, this time everything was handled as swiftly and silently as could be managed. There was some minor coverage in the local papers that Paul Knowles was being jailed for kidnapping, but all of the details were kept carefully under wraps. As a result, the time that he faced in jail for the solitary crime he was being charged with was actually relatively short, to avoid drawing unwanted attention. And Paul was placed into a relatively low-security prison on the basis that they did not want him interacting with any of the more hardened criminals who might learn from him exactly how and why he had been arrested. Some part of this was, of course, collusion between the police and the court, but a distinct influence was also the fact that Paul looked relatively innocent and confused about the whole thing. As though he had acted on a foolish impulse and now felt suitably embarrassed.

It was strange to think that someone could appear innocent when they stood trial for abducting a police officer at gunpoint, but the narratives from both his lawyer and the police lined up perfectly. The victim even gave a sworn statement on the stand emphasizing how little hostility he'd actually experienced from the young man. The markedly soft sentence was the first criminal record to be officially attached to young Paul, and it set the tone for all of his interactions with the courts in the future. All it took was a glance back at this record and they would know that he was to be treated with kid gloves.

He served out his sentence in relative obscurity, sullenly doing whatever he was told whenever he was told and hating every single moment of it, but still aware that it was the best way to survive. Now that he had actually committed a crime worth mentioning, he had gone into prison fully expecting to suffer markedly worse treatment than he had received at what had ostensibly been a school for troublesome youths. What he found instead was a holiday. He didn't have to scrape and scramble to put money in his pocket and food in his mouth when he was imprisoned. He didn't have to find a place to sleep each night. The other low-security prisoners were not the hardened monsters that Dozier had made out of all the other boys entrusted to them. There was no risk of murder or rape. In truth, the place barely seemed like a punishment at all. He still longed for the freedom of the road and all of the hedonistic pleasures that it brought him, but that was the same way that a child longed for ice cream for every meal. He'd been indulging himself so wildly when he was in the outside world that his time in prison served almost like a cleanse to bring him back to reality.

There was no long arduous turn of years as he waited to be freed from his confinement. No trying desperately to work out when his next birthday would come and set him loose. Just a few months locked away with some minimal supervision to make sure he wasn't getting up to any particularly dangerous mischief, and then he was let out onto the street again the same as before.

He had committed three crimes by the end of that first day, breaking and entering, burglary, and grand theft auto. Then he was back on the road with a wallet full of cash, a box full of thrift shop clothes, and as close to a new car as he'd risk stealing.

He got out of town fast, before anyone might connect the newly released convict with the sudden crime spree, but he really shouldn't have bothered. The burglaries and petty thefts he'd committed prior to his arrest were largely forgotten by the time he started up again, and when he moved along to the next town, his deeds were soon forgotten again. Barely even a blip in the local crime reports.

So his life went on, and the years rolled by. He would be picked up by the police repeatedly in the years to come and gave himself over to them freely each time without a hint of an attempt to resist. He had learned his lesson from that very first arrest—if he went along with whatever they said and acted polite, then they'd let him off easy every single time. He was so personable with the police that they found themselves freely chatting with him as though he was a friend. He was encountering new officers each time, thanks to his nomadic tendencies, and while inter-department communication was getting marginally better across state lines, more often than not when he was charged with a crime it was treated as though it was his first offence because the appropriate paperwork was nowhere to be seen. Even when it was, all a judge had to do was look back on the lenient sentences Paul had been previously given to know that he wasn't any real trouble, just a silly kid caught up in things at the wrong time.

Sometimes he'd be caught in the midst of a burglary. Sometimes he'd be caught in a stolen car. There is no question that he should have been imprisoned for a damn sight longer than he ever was. It seems that across the many states he chose to prey on, his easy-going attitude and boyish manner, throwing up his hands and saying 'whoops, you caught me', turned out to be sufficiently endearing to the police that no real consequences for his actions ever fully caught up with him before he was on the move again. Repeat offenders were meant to suffer more serious punishments for their crimes, yet all the way through to 1970 he was rarely behind bars for more than a few months stint at a time. Admittedly, due to the sheer number of times that he was arrested in those years, he still spent more time imprisoned than free, but the fact that he was set loose to commit further crimes is a testament to just how gently the criminal justice system seemed intent on treating him.

From 1970 on, however, that began to change. By this point, the boyish charm was starting to fade from Paul, and systems for the sharing of information across counties and states were improving. The frankly ridiculous length of the list of convictions against him became known to the judges he was throwing himself on the mercy of, and at the same time, mandatory sentencing reforms meant that they could no longer let him off lightly when it was abundantly clear that he was a career criminal. The low-security prisons gave way to high-security prisons, and then finally when he was arrested in 1971 for yet another burglary, one in which he'd entered a home while the resident was present and had to tie them up to ensure they wouldn't interfere in his work, it was taken as a sign that he was escalating to new levels of violence and becoming a real danger to others. He was sentenced to a hefty three years, to be served doing hard labour in a work camp, instead of the cushy holidays that he had been weathering so easily so far.

If they expected it to shock him and put him back on the straight and narrow, then they were sorely mistaken. Instead, he took a different lesson from the experience. Not that committing crimes was wrong and would result in negative consequences for him, but that now that the punishment was starting to become more of an inconvenience to him, it was time to start actively resisting it and avoiding capture.

While he was delivered to the work camp in 1972, he had no intention of staying there for the full length of his sentence this time around. With the tools and equipment available to him during the day, he fashioned a set of lockpicks for himself, and when night fell and he was locked away, he made quick work of the cell door and then strolled right out. Guards weren't stationed to watch the perimeter through the night because all of the prisoners were locked down. It was a bit of a hike back to civilization, and he had to make do with his prison uniform until such time as he could lay his hands on some regular clothes, but it didn't take him long. He had to go straight into burglary without the usual intermediate stage of shoplifting and petty theft, but once he was done, he was back to his usual state of being in no time at all. A case of clothes, a wallet full of cash, and a stolen car to carry him off to the next place along the highway.

The alarm wasn't even raised until he was long gone, when the guards went to haul him out of his cell in the morning for breakfast and found the door hanging open.

At which point all hell broke loose.

A freed prisoner strolling off to commit further crimes was essentially expected by this point, but a prisoner that had broken out of a high-security prison was both a danger to the public and, more pressingly, an embarrassment to those in power.

A manhunt was underway, and all of the usual low-level incompetence that made living life easy for men like Paul was burned away in the heat of the spotlight being shone on the police force. Every crime that he committed was logged, compared to his past behaviour, and became another breadcrumb for investigators to follow. His picture was sent out ahead of him to all of the towns he was expected to hit once the geographical pattern of his escape route was identified.

As he came flying along the highway without a care in the world or a worry in his mind, it all came crashing down. There was a blockade set up ahead of him, stopping and checking each car as it went by. He didn't have a licence to show them, and even if he did, his face was still the one that they were looking for. He spun the car into a full U-turn across the motorway and went tearing off right into the waiting snare of the police who had been trundling along behind him since he'd left the last town. He was caught in a trap, and there was no way out for him.

As was usual for him when he was confronted with an impossible situation, he just went with the flow, turning off the car and stepping out with his arms raised and a smile on his face. He did not get the usual smiles of relief from the arresting officers nor did he get the gentle treatment to which he was accustomed. They knelt on his back as they fastened the handcuffs, and when he let out a cry of dismay, he was treated to a bludgeoning blow around the back of the head.

There would be no free roaming or access to tools this time around. Nor would there be any more of the soft treatment that he had been receiving up until now. He was marked by the guards in Raiford Prison as trouble after tales of his previous escape reached them, and while other convicts could breathe easy around them, there wasn't a moment that Paul wasn't kept under their watchful eyes. Knowing that if they gave him an inch he'd take a mile, they gave Paul nothing, not even enough space to turn his head without somebody questioning why he was doing it. For a man who cherished his freedom so much, it was the worst kind of torment. Like being back in his father's house, having to account for every minute decision he made, every noise he let out. He was in hell, and to his mounting horror, he realised that he'd had worse. Even the worst punishments that the government could hand down to him, even the tightest shackles that they could place upon his wrists, were still like a slap on the wrist compared to what he had already endured.

They were already treating him as badly as they could possibly manage without breaking their own rules, which meant that there was no punishment worse that could be inflicted on him. He had nothing to lose and so became ungovernable.

So, it was with this in mind, that the prison administration set out to give him something to lose. Not his freedom, which was already forfeit, not kind treatment, which he would never trust, but some tie to the real world beyond the walls of the institution where he was bound, some reason to seek rehabilitation instead of punishment. All that it would take was one real human connection to form a lever that could be used to pry him out of the pits of depravity into which he was sunk.

The Heart Uncaged

The guards were instructed to ease off the pressure on Paul, though they were loath to do so, and in so doing allowed him measures of free time throughout his day in which to amuse himself. Some prisoners would have used that time to work on themselves. Some would have spent it looking for escape through books or television. Paul did not do anything. He had no hobbies or interests, nothing in his life except the moment in which he lived. The same thing that made him immune to threats of punishment made him incapable of generating joy for himself. This was a problem for the guards. If there was nothing that he liked, there was nothing that they could take away from him when he disobeyed. A rethink was required.

It would be necessary not to find the things he loved, but to instil a love of something in him.

From the early days of his imprisonment, it was apparent that the usual prison friendships that could be relied upon to spring up were not going to happen for Paul. He had never had much interest in friendship, only adoration, and in this state prison, he was a small fish in a big pond—not his preferred fish-to-pond-size ratio. Nobody knew who he was, and nobody cared.

He couldn't have the spotlight, so he made no effort to sidle on stage.

A friendship with another prisoner wouldn't have been ideal, but it at least would have been a starting point. Instead, it seemed they were going to have to look further afield.

Which was why, when the prison pen-pal programme opened up for new applicants, a note about it had been left in his cell when he returned from his work duty and he was certain to have nothing to do.

With nothing better to do with his time, Paul signed up and began sending letters back and forth with a variety of people. It broke up the monotony of his day, brought in some news from the outside, and provided the guards with a small but tangible threat to use against him. If he wanted his mail, he'd behave himself.

Given that there was no real reason to rail against his captors, Paul did what he did best: He went with the flow.

Over his months of incarceration, his correspondents began to whittle down, with many of them losing interest or moving on from the dark places in their own lives that had left them so desperate for human interaction that they turned to the prison population for their social needs. Yet one persisted, and her letters became transformative for Paul.

To him, love had always been a trap—the snare that kept you in place while you were bludgeoned by the ones who supposedly loved you. Yet the feelings that he was beginning to develop towards his pen-pal came with no sense of obligation, no demands. Love in those letters seemed less like bait in a trap and more like a prize.

For the first time in his life, he found himself talking to a woman as though she were a human being rather than a tool to pleasure himself with. There was no possibility of a physical consummation of their relationship—not when he was locked behind bars—and she was states away on the other coast of the continent. Instead of just trotting out whatever trite lies would get him closer to his end goal of spreading her legs, he found himself telling the truth about himself. Not the whole of it, of course—he didn't want to scare her away and be left bereft of company—but enough that she came to know at least some of the real him. It was a unique experience for Paul, who'd had it beaten into him from birth that he was unworthy of love and affection for who he was, and only by creating brief illusions of normalcy might he receive even a moment of affection.

He lied about the crime that he had committed, pretending it was a drug charge rather than burglary, acting as though he were a victim of circumstance rather than the creator of his own situation. It was a lie of omission more than anything else, the kind of casual self-delusion that helped most of his fellow inmates through the day. He was aware that it was a deception, of course. He was always aware of what he was doing, and why. That hyper-awareness of his own actions and motives had been beaten into him, too.

But barring the slight edit of history to make himself seem less of a danger, the rest of his conversations with Angela Covic reflected his real philosophies on life. The joy of freedom, trusting fate, living without fear. It was intensely appealing to someone who had spent her life constrained by one controlling man after another. A demanding father had led Angela to marry early to an equally controlling man, and now as her marriage began to crumble, the possibility of a life without all of the rules that had bound her had to sound more appealing. The man who offered her that life was attractive by default.

At this point, with the more violent or cruel elements of his story curtailed, the handsome Paul looked every bit like the kind of counter-culture rebel that Angela had grown up admiring, safe and neutered behind bars so he could be adored and appreciated without any real danger. The perfect bad boy.

She fell for him, and fell for him hard, but as surprising as that might have been, the fact that he seemed to feel exactly the same way about her was all the more inconceivable. This was a man who did not believe that love existed, or that if it did, it took only the form of a tyrant swinging it like a whip to control his vassals. At no point in his life had he ever encountered a relationship like this, yet despite having no map, he rushed out into the undiscovered country, trusting fate as he did on the road.

The couple built their rapport over literally hundreds of letters, flitting back and forth every single day, both of them oh-so gradually exposing more and more of their feelings for the other. Paul falling in love for the first time, Angela falling in love with the fantasy that she had made Paul the central player of.

The relationship continued to escalate despite Angela clearly recognizing that things were getting out of hand. She knew better. She had a lifetime of experience with men to tell her that if things seemed too good to be true, they probably were. That the romance faded and all that was left in the cold light of day was the awful weight of obligation. Yet she could not let go of her fantasy. She followed it onto a Greyhound bus, all the way across the United States of America to arrive in Florida one morning just before visiting hours at the state prison.

When she finally saw him, through the plate glass, she couldn't believe her eyes. She had thought that he had sent along an old photo, or that it had been the one good picture of him. She had no idea that he was actually going to be that handsome in real life. Nor could she have predicted the way that when his eyes met hers, it would send sparks shooting down her spine. Her bad boy. Her Paul. Just the thought of it left her jittery. They were still held apart by the glass, but he was close enough to touch. Her head felt like it was spinning. She could really have this, have him. All she had to do was keep saying yes. All she had to was say yes, and he could be her whole world.

She could barely remember the conversation afterwards. She could remember the way that the light shone across his face and the way the corner of his mouth quirked up when she spoke. She could remember the perfect aquiline of his nose and the way his eyebrows rose each time that he saw her. They had spoken about things, things that had probably mattered once upon a time, but that was before, and this was now. Now she had seen him in all his glory. And all she had to do was say yes.

With his eyes bright and teary, he rose from his seat and went down onto one knee. It was like all the air left the room. Those words she could still remember when she left the prison. Those soft-spoken entreaties to spend the rest of their life together, making each other better, sharing kindness in a world that was anything but kind. She could remember her own words, too, the ones that she had blurted out without a second thought when he asked her to marry him. The word that she had to say. The one she just had to keep saying.

Yes.

In an instant, Paul was transformed. Up until now, he'd been edging closer and closer to being a model prisoner as a result of his new letter-writing fixation, but now the change was apparent to everyone. He no longer cared about life in the prison, no longer cared about appearances. There was something out there that was worth living for. Worth winning his freedom for. He was in love, and the woman that he loved had announced to the world that she loved him right back. It changed everything.

If things had turned out differently, this would have been the turning point where his life changed track, where he left prison and became a law-abiding member of society. But things would not turn out differently because there were factors entirely beyond the control of Paul Knowles at work.

To the casual observer, it might have seemed that their whirlwind romance was the usual cold and calculating manipulation that criminals often inflicted upon the soft-hearted women of the world, but in all things, it seemed that Angela was the active agent. She was the one who had announced she was making the cross-country journey to meet him. She was the one who committed to his proposal after planting the seeds for it in her letters with conversation about the importance of marriage to her. While you might have expected Paul to be twisting her to his will, the opposite was in fact the case. She was changing him. Day by day. Making him into a more appropriate husband than the jailbird that he was. It was her who had the bright idea to hire a lawyer to look over the details of his conviction. He had never even considered challenging his sentence to be a possibility. In his mind, there was no challenging authority, just enduring the punishments it doled out, seemingly at random.

With Sheldon Yavitz in his corner for the first time, it soon became apparent that there were a great many holes in the case that had been brought against him. Client–attorney privilege kept his fiancée in the dark about the real charges against him, while that same attorney did frankly amazing work combing over every detail of his conviction and arrest to find the tiny errors in police work that would allow the case to be overturned.

A sentence that was meant to last for nearly a decade abruptly ended, and all of Angela Covic's fantasies suddenly leapt from the realm of dream into reality in a single moment.

She panicked.

As a romantic dream, being engaged to Paul had served her well and filled her with excitement, but now that tipped over into roiling anxiety as she had to face what day-to-day life with him would be like. She had been in relationship after relationship, always looking for 'the one'. Always searching for the next great romance that would magically fix every problem in her life. Paul had been perfect in the abstract, and so long as their relationship remained an abstraction, she would not have to face up to the fact that it could not be everything that she needed.

Paul got out of jail and straight onto a bus to San Francisco. She got the call from his lawyer with the times and dates. The moments were ticking down until he arrived.

In a state of considerable distress and agitation, Angela sought out guidance. She needed a sign from the universe that things were going to work out, that Paul was going to be the man that completed her and made all things right again. She did not turn to her friends, whom she knew would immediately tell her the truth about just how insane she had been in prying a man out of prison to come cross-country and be her new husband. She did not turn to her family because how could she when they all believed that she was still happily married? Instead, she reached out to a more esoteric source for advice. Her psychic.

There was no shortage of crystal balls and tarot cards in San Francisco, but there was only one woman that Angela trusted—the one psychic who had guided her through all of the troubles that had beset her life as a result of cruel fate, and definitely not as a result of her own terrible decisions.

So when she settled down to receive guidance from her higher self, Gods, angels or whoever else came along, and her beloved psychic's face twisted into a mask of faux horror, she already knew that she'd made a mistake.

The prediction that she received that day would not only change the course of her own life, but that of dozens of others. A tall dark stranger was coming into her life. A dangerous man. There were other parts to the prediction, parts that she missed out on as those words reverberated in her mind. A dangerous man. A stranger. All the things that she feared Paul was going to be bubbled up to overwhelm her.

When he arrived on her doorstep with his gas-station flower bouquet in hand, he was expecting to be welcomed in with open arms. He didn't even make it past the welcome mat. The wedding was off. The engagement was off. Their relationship was at its end. He couldn't understand what was happening. He couldn't understand how things could have changed so dramatically in the time since their last letter.

She closed the door in his face, turned around and fell back into her husband's waiting arms. This had been the testing point of a marriage in decline, their last chance to turn things around. To see her as desirable to other men was enough of a shock to her husband that he mended his ways. Enough that they put in the extra work that was required to repair their relationship, at least to a sufficient enough degree that their marriage lurched on for a few years afterwards.

It's easy to look at these events with hindsight and say that Angela Covic dodged a bullet on that day. Equally, it is easy to heap blame on her, for offering a man hope and then snatching it away, ripping apart the first semblance of a healthy relationship that he had ever experienced. She could not have known what kind of man she was setting loose on the world any more than the world could have known what she would have suffered had she been the one to keep all of Paul's behaviour behind closed doors. She made her decision, supposedly informed by the wisdom of the spiritual world, and there is no way to know how life would have unfolded otherwise.

Paul went berserk.

Just as she had built him up to be the fantasy man of her dreams, so too had he viewed her through the same rose-tinted glasses. She was his saviour. The one that he would pull himself up from the lowest circles of hell to be with. The conscience that he never had. The heart that he had never grown. In short, he expected her to take care of the complex business of emotions for him, and all of his problems would be resolved by a hug and a kiss on the cheek. She could not be his saviour. She could not even be another one of the girls that he had sated his passions on through the years, because she was too pure and perfect. She was the Madonna to their Whores.

It is at this point that Paul John Knowles' story diverges from that which is supported by the evidence. That is not to say that his depiction of events is untrue, only that sufficient proof has never been produced to corroborate his version of events. For the sake of completeness, his version of events will be included in this account, but it is important to understand that they have not been substantiated fully.

According to Paul, that was the night of his first murder. He was so enraged at the cruel rejection by his one true love that he took to the streets of San Francisco to seek vengeance on the world that had spurned him.

That very night he stalked through the shadowy side streets of the City by the Bay with mad murderous intent, slaughtering not one, not two, but three separate people. Screaming out his vengeance into the night.

If all of this seems a little theatrical, it is probably worth mentioning that Paul was a big fan of the movies growing up—sneaking in to see them at every opportunity as a child and making pit stops in his cross-country touring whenever there was a new release that caught his fancy. He expressed on many occasions that he wanted to be an actor, that he had the looks for the silver screen, that he wanted fame above all else. When the time came to tell his own story, he seemed to be pitching it like a scriptwriter to a producer. Giving the elements that lacked flair a little bit of a polish. Establishing himself as the victim of cruel circumstance, a tragic Byronic hero who had love snatched from his grasping hands and sought vengeance against the whole cruel world as a result.

There were in fact murders in San Francisco around the date that he was there, several of which could have been perpetrated by him, but the lack of detail in his descriptions of events left the police with no way to confirm or deny his involvement with any one of them.

The next time that the story solidified back into fact was the following day, when the supposedly distraught and murderous Paul wandered back to Angela's doorstep like he was a lost puppy and made such mournful noises that she took pity on him. For all that she claimed to see an 'aura of fear' around him, she still felt guilty about dragging him across the country under what turned out to be false pretences. At the same time, she was obviously under some pressure from her husband to be rid of the ex-con lingering around outside as swiftly as possible. He was even willing to foot the bill for the plane ticket that would send Paul soaring back across the map to Florida, out of their lives, out of their minds, and out of the way of any consequences that might arise from his supposed murder spree on the previous night.

Running Wild

Paul was free. He had the whole world rolled out like a red carpet at his feet. Everything that he claimed to want from life, he had, yet he was not happy. His brief dalliance with the possibility of love and a regular life seemed to have soured him to the life that he'd enjoyed before.

Where before he had faced life with reckless abandon, now he seemed to consider the world to be his enemy, actively working against him and his happiness. He felt like he needed to fight for every ounce of joy that he could get, and if anyone stood in his way, then he unleashed his impressive temper on them.

Gone were the happy stories of his passage through the towns of Florida, where he'd stop in just long enough to meet a girl, have something to drink, and then be on his merry way again. Now he lingered, and he didn't have a few drinks—he aimed to consume the whole bar before his tab was called. Where before he had driven away from his problems to escape them, now he drank to escape from himself. It wasn't enough. It was never enough. No matter how much he drank, he could still remember the cold shame of standing on Angela's doorstep and being rejected. She was everything he'd thought he could never have, dangled in front of him like a carrot on a stick, and he'd gone running across the whole world trying to catch it, even though it would always be out of reach. Of course, he couldn't have it. He wasn't deserving of love. He wasn't deserving of anything but unjust punishment heaped on unjust punishment. He'd rarely hurt anybody so badly they couldn't walk it off. He'd never robbed somebody that couldn't stand to lose a little cash. He didn't follow the letter of the law, but he'd never actually done something that he truly considered bad. He broke the rules when he thought the rules were stupid, but he had never crossed the line that so many of his fellow prisoners had. In his heart of hearts, he still believed that he was the hero of the story.

In the mire of drunken fury, that changed. He lost sight of who he was, what he was, who he wanted to be. He retreated back inside himself from the edge of humanity where he had been dipping his toes in and considering a paddle.

He had been hurt. All of this time, he had never truly felt hurt thanks to hiding out in his own mind like it was a snail's shell. Bad things had happened to him, but he had been able to hold onto the idea that they were random cruelties, things that could be endured until he got past them to freedom and joy again. But with his attempt to pursue a normal life, he had left himself open to normal strife. So long as he never tried, he could never fail. So long as he never put his real feelings out there, they could never be hurt.

He had allowed himself, if only for a short time, to believe that he could have the things that everyone else had, and that poisoned his joy now. It no longer felt like he was making a brave choice to be different and free, to have what others could not. It felt like the open road, the drinking and a different woman in every town, were the consolation prize after he'd failed at being a normal human being. It felt like losing.

Paul did not like that feeling. So he drank to forget it. When he was drunk enough, he could forget all about everything and just feel good like he used to. That was always the goal, to get back to the way he was before. To put all thoughts of love and marriage and picket fences out of his mind and go back to the nothing he'd always been. Hurting nobody, loved by nobody, gone before the sun came up.

Unfortunately, the drink didn't just dampen down the memories that hurt him, they silenced that little voice in his head telling him that he was meant to be the hero of this movie. In trying to forget who he was, he forgot who he was meant to be.

So, when a bartender in Southern Florida stomped over to demand payment after Paul had spent a solid twelve hours demolishing the beer supply in his fine roadside establishment, shouting at him and calling him names, the little voice of reason that usually stood between the real world and the roiling hate and fury inside of him was not there.

This was not the first time that this particular bartender had dealt with a rowdy customer. It was not an upscale establishment where there was never any fighting. In fact, he fully expected this strange loner to take a swing at him before the day was done. It was almost part of the social contract that drunken strangers made an attempt at violence before giving in and paying up. The difference was that usually the decision was made through the haze of booze with tectonic slowness. Usually, he could see the thought percolating, the expression changing, the weight of the drunk's body getting shifted into position for a punch. It was an easy part of the job to step aside, to let them wear themselves out or to return a jab or two to put them back on the straight and narrow.

When Paul moved, it wasn't like that. It was like there were no intermediate steps between the thought of violence and the action. Like his body obeyed some deeper command than those of thoughts. He was up from his seat and into motion like a cobra striking, and before the bartender could even bring his hands up to protect his head, the knife that had somehow sprung into Paul's hand had slipped in between his ribs.

It was only then, with hot blood oozing out onto his hand, that Paul seemed to realise what he had done. He blinked and seemed to realise what he was looking at a moment after. From inches away the bartender finally got to see the shift in emotions on his face, from the blank mask he had been presenting before to surprise, then horror at what he had done. Even as the bartender's legs gave out, Paul was in motion again, tugging out the knife, tossing it aside and catching the man before he fell, lowering him gingerly down onto the filthy floor of the bar with a jabbering attempt at an apology on his lips.

He had never meant to hurt anybody again. Never meant to take all the pain that he was feeling and turn it out into one sharp point and bury it into somebody else. That wasn't who he wanted to be… until now.

There was literally blood on his hands. And it just got worse as he tried to apply pressure to the wound and stop the flow of red. The other patrons of the bar came charging over, dragged him off the poor barman, and hit Paul around the face a few times until they felt sure he wasn't going to go lunging after his victim again. Only then did they spring into action, calling for an ambulance, and police, stuffing the filthy rag that was used to wipe glasses into the hole in the poor barman's side to try and stop the great gouts of blood that were escaping still.

Paul let it all happen. He didn't try to fight back or break free. He didn't try to run before the police could arrive. He just stood there, as pale-faced as the man lying bleeding on the floor, looking twice as hurt to find that his own body, the one thing that he'd always thought of as his own, could take such drastic action without consulting him. Instinct had come out at that moment, and as it turned out, he had the instincts of a killer.

There was not even the faintest hint of the usual joviality that Paul faced when the police arrested him. There was no thrill of the chase for either party. He had not run, hadn't moved an inch from where the other patrons sat him. Paul looked so devastated by the time that they got him to the station that they actually called in a doctor to check him over and confirm that none of the blood was his. It wasn't.

When he went to trial, he didn't even try to mount a defence even though he now had a fairly decent lawyer on his side thanks to the efforts of Angela Covic. Why would he, when he felt that his actions were indefensible? Why would he, when he didn't even feel like he had made the decisions that led to his arrest? One by one, the different patrons of the bar came up to the box and gave their testimony. He'd attacked the man for no reason at all. He hadn't hesitated for a moment. Even after he'd stabbed him, that wasn't enough violence. He'd followed the poor barman to the ground. The only witness who wasn't called was the barman himself. He'd survived the injuries, but the prosecution had decided that his testimony wouldn't add anything to their case, confused as it was. Not to mention that by keeping him out of sight of the jury, they could give the distinct impression that this was a murder trial, even if that wasn't strictly the case.

To a man, the other patrons spoke about the needless brutality of Paul's actions. The suddenness of his violence. None of them, in the chaos, had realised Paul's immediate guilt, or that he had been making attempts to help his victim. For his part, Paul assumed that they did know and were lying to see him punished. He couldn't even bring himself to get angry about it. After all, he was guilty. He had done exactly what they said he'd done. He'd lashed out and hurt somebody for no good reason at all. The brutality of it left him shocked and appalled the same as them. The only difference was that it had been his hand holding the knife, his body moving of its own volition to fight back against the bully looming over him. Like the shadow of his father.

The jury agreed with everyone's assessment that Paul needed to be locked up, and the judge was quick to pass down as lengthy a sentence as it was possible to give for such a crime. The only thing that prevented a life sentence was the general agreement that the crime had not been in any way premeditated, and the fact that his victim had survived the experience. If there had been any way that the lawyers and witnesses could have made it seem like Paul was guilty of first-degree murder, then that would no doubt have been the case that they made, but no amount of massaging the facts could make it so that a drifter coming into a town at random had plans to kill a stranger ahead of time over a bar tab he hadn't even run up yet.

With his sentencing complete, Paul was hauled back to his cell, from there to be transferred to state prison and serve out as long a sentence as it was possible for him to serve before parole might be offered. The last deal to get him out of jail had been more-or-less a trade to get him out on parole instead of dragging the whole of the courts through the muck and trouble, but that meant that his previously unserved time would be added on top of this sentence, too. He was going to be in jail for a very long time. Not the short stints he'd been able to shrug off before. Not the endless summers of his desecrated childhood. He was facing the distinct possibility that he would never see the world outside of prison again.

After being tossed into his cell, Paul didn't make a sound, didn't speak to Sheldon Yavitz when the man came by with big talk of mistrials and appeals, didn't even acknowledge the guards when they banged on his door and slid him the slop they considered to be dinner. His mind was turned inward, his thoughts swirling about as he tried to make sense of everything that had happened.

This was not how his story was meant to play out. He was meant to be a movie star, not a convict. He was a bad boy, not an evil man. The script of his life had been flipped in one moment when his body had leapt into motion to protect him from a danger that just wasn't there. That bartender was not trying to hurt him. He wasn't one of the Dozier guards, another prisoner intent on robbing or raping him. He wasn't his father with belt in hand, either. The ghosts of all those monsters from long ago may have fogged his mind momentarily when Paul leapt to his feet, but he had just been a man, going to work, living out his little life as guiltlessly as anybody could.

How could Paul pretend that he was a good man after stabbing another good man in the guts for having the temerity to ask him to pay his tab?

He couldn't. There was no way to cling to that golden image of himself, perfect and benevolent, in the face of what he'd done. Who he thought he was, was gone. Who he really was remained to be discovered. And alone in that cell as the sun went down, Paul turned his mind to that question. Who was he now, after the things that had been done to him throughout the years, and the things that he had done himself? Who was he?

The totality of that answer was beyond his reach at that moment. Indeed, it seems quite likely that he never fully got the chance at introspection that would be required to uncover that answer at all. But some small parts of it, he could address.

As guilty as he might have felt about the impromptu stabbing, it was not enough to justify his losing his whole life. His heart might be hurting from the rejection that he'd suffered, and he might still need some time to get his head around the idea that he had even wanted a normal life, settled down with some lady, but that same heart was still beating, each heartbeat pumping hedonistic blood throughout his body.

There would be no joy in prison. No freedom. Not even the false versions that he was now convinced he'd been indulging in since he was cut loose from Dozier. Everything would be the same dull concrete, the same tasteless food, the same miserable faces. There would be nothing worth living for in there if there were no promise of escape at the other end of it.

For the very first time, it seemed to sink into his head why it was that other men feared prison, why they obeyed the strictures of the law, so that they could still pretend at freedom. And it was that fear that drove him to stir from where he lay in the jail cell on the side of the courthouse. It was that fear that guided his quaking fingers and the stolen paperclips that he'd lifted from his lawyer's useless folder to the lock on the outside of the barred door. It was harder to pick a lock like this, unable to see it, ears pricked up for any hint of a patrolling guard, but hard as it might have been, he still managed it. Tumbler by tumbler, inch by inch, he unlocked the door to his cell. It was only when everything was lined up perfectly and he started to twist the old lock open that his makeshift lockpicks snapped.

They weren't dense enough to take the weight of the ancient lock. He had beaten the mechanism and halfway turned the lock, but the weight of the metal inside had been too much for the paperclips to handle. He tried to compact the remains that he had left in his aching fingers into a single piece that he might use, but try as he might, he couldn't get through the metal that he had already jammed into the lock. It wasn't fair. He'd done everything right, and he was still going to get carted off to eternal misery. It wasn't fair! Rearing back, he kicked at the door with all his fury, and it popped open.

The lock had been stiff. All it had needed was a solid whack to get it to finish turning the rest of the way.

Of course, any hope of a quiet escape had been thoroughly ruined by the bang and clatter of his final fury at lock manufacturers everywhere. Cursing himself for a fool, he ran out, grabbing what he could on the way, ducking out of sight when the night-watch passed him by, until he made it out into the balmy Florida air and the chirruping of grasshoppers. At last, his frantic scurry stopped, and he took in a deep breath.

Things were going to be harder from here on out. There would be no more taking things lightly, and there could be no more playing at being a criminal like it was a game. Everywhere he'd gone before, he had left a trail behind him like he was just another idiot. He'd known that the things he did could be traced back to him, but he'd always assumed that folks were too busy getting on with their own lives to try and come together to witch-hunt him for trying to live better. But he knew better now. The seeds of paranoia were planted after that whole bar full of people had turned out to damn him even though he hadn't even meant to hurt the man. One by one, they'd looked down their noses at him from up in the witness box and said that he was an animal that needed to be caged. That he was a beast running wild.

Well, there would be no more running wild. The time had come to start thinking things through, planning his next move and relying on his own logic to guide him instead of kowtowing to what he'd once thought was the right thing to do. He'd tried to do the right thing in that bar, and look at the parade of betrayal it had bought him. He'd tried to be the good guy, the star, the heartthrob. He'd done his part and followed the script, and nothing had worked out the way that he wanted. He'd kissed the girl and the credits hadn't rolled on their happily ever after. He had been robbed of that. And now they were trying to rob him of what little solace he had left in this world.

They wanted to cage him? He'd rather die.

He took off in a full pelt run from outside of the prison feeling the night air on his skin, feeling the burn of his muscles. He was free, and this time around, he meant to stay that way. No more foolish mistakes. No more letting his instincts take over. Everything had to be planned. Every loose end had to be tied off. If he couldn't be the hero of this piece, then he was certain that he wasn't going to be the repentant villain, paying for his crimes with his life. If they wanted him to be bad, then he'd be so good at it that the world would remember his name forever.

It was in the early hours of July 26, 1974, that Paul walked free. And within twenty-four hours, he would deliberately kill for the first time.

RYAN GREEN

Unfortunate Events

The first thought on Paul's mind was escape. He could still recall the last time that he had broken out of police custody and the ensuing dragnet. He had no intention of being caught up in it again, which meant that he had to get out of Dodge as quickly as possible. Ideally before the sun rose.

He had decided to be more of a thinking man, so he addressed the situation logically. He needed a car to get away. But a car would only carry him so far on whatever was left in the tank. So really, he needed a car and money. A change of clothes wouldn't go amiss either, since any APB that the police put out would include details of his current attire. Stealing a car was simple enough, but money and clothes required a burglary, something that this newly cerebral version of Paul knew was not a matter to be rushed. Ideally, a good burglary would take days, studying the property, the best way to gain access, the best time to break in when nobody would be around. Even scouting out the best possibilities could take up to a week. He had hours. This meant that to have any hope of success, he was going to have to start breaking some of his own rules. It was true that he'd always been fairly relaxed when it came to setting restrictions on himself, but even a free spirit had common sense. He never committed a burglary without the right equipment, he never did it when he couldn't be sure the house was empty, he never did it anywhere that could be connected back to him.

That last one had always come easy. Of course it had. Nowhere was connected to him and nobody was, either. At least that was how things normally were during his endless rambling. But he was in Jacksonville now, the same town his mother lived in, where he had come by to visit once in a while during his excursions. Where some of his brothers and sisters were, too. He might not know them to look at them, but he was damned sure that the police would go straight to them once his absence from his cell was noted, and that meant that going anywhere near to them was tantamount to handing himself back over.

Yet, the low-rent neighbourhood that his mother called home was the only bit of Jacksonville that he'd spent any time scouting out for soft targets— something he probably shouldn't have done, but by this point in his criminal career was pretty much habitual. He could think of a few places that would turn up what he needed, a few homes that could serve as his piggy bank and dressing room, and offer up a set of car keys, to boot. Life was always easier with keys than with a hotwired car. Just like the change of clothes, it wouldn't change the fact that he was a wanted man, but it would help him to pass for normal. It would let people be taken in by his charisma instead of getting hung up on stupid little details like a blatantly stolen car or the fact that he was wearing a prison uniform.

There was a clock ticking down in his head to the moment the guard would realize that he was gone. Until the cops were called in. Until they could get organised enough to start hunting him. He'd set a mental deadline of daybreak to get the hell out of Jacksonville, but in truth every minute that he lingered made his odds of escape all the worse. Everything was a trade-off.

Cash, car, clothes. They were worth swapping an extra hour for. They'd be the difference between getting out before the roadblocks were up, keeping on going past the limits they would have imagined for him, and for passing by any suspicious cops that had heard about him over the radio. He needed them. So he was going to take them.

The house he had in mind was a small one, home to only a single resident, an old woman that he figured spent maybe half the year there and the other half off staying in hospitals or with family. The usual neighbourhood rumours could have filled him in on more if he'd had the time to scout things out properly—give him dates and times and some sense of what he was walking into—but just like the hour that he was trading, Paul decided to roll the dice and hope for the best. The situation wasn't perfect, and it wasn't like he couldn't handle some old lady. He'd screwed up in situations just like this before and ended up perfectly fine. Bit of rope. A chair. She could just sit there until morning when somebody came looking for her to work out why she'd never turned up for coffee or bridge or whatever the hell you did when all hope of sex was a distant memory. It would give her a scare, but that was the worst-case scenario. It wasn't like he was going to hurt her, or even put the fear in her like he'd had to do to the last guy. Everything was going to be fine.

He went through his usual circuit of the place, but the distant sound of sirens spooked him before he could get a good look inside, and he had to switch tactics. Without his usual picks, he wouldn't be able to break in cleanly, so he put his elbow through the glass pane of the back door and let himself in. It was louder than he'd have liked, but honestly, it was probably better to make the noise now and find out somebody was in the building than to be surprised by it when he went wandering into a bedroom.

No alarm went off, which was a good thing, but not entirely good. Old ladies living alone normally swore by alarms. So if there wasn't one beeping in his ear, that might mean she wasn't off visiting.

He had his targets fixed in mind. Car keys would be somewhere in the hall. Valuables in drawers. Change of clothes stowed away in closets. Hopefully, the old woman had a husband once upon a time and had been sentimental enough to hold onto some of his shirts. Showing up in the next town over wearing a frilly sundress probably wouldn't help him blend in all that well. He smirked in the dark at the thought of it. He was standing there, reaching for the door to the hall, when it swung open and the light switch was flicked on.

Alice Curtis had heard a noise downstairs. Nothing too alarming, just a clatter like a plate had fallen over. Odds were one of the neighbours' cats had gotten stuck inside the house again. It happened every summer. The doors stood open all day to keep the muggy air flowing through, and wouldn't you know, some manner of beast always made its way inside to find a shady patch for a nap. She supposed she was lucky she didn't live out in the bayou, where you were more likely to find a gator than a kitty on your doorstep, pawing to get in for some dinner.

So, you can imagine her surprise when she opened up the kitchen door, turned on the lights, and came face to face with the Devil himself—like something out of the crime magazines she liked to read, an escaped convict grinning at her like he was an old friend. Alice was only sixty-five years old, and her heart was still going strong, but her legs still gave a little at the sight of him. She toppled back, and then he was on her, pouncing forward like a puma to catch her before she could fall, lowering her down onto the floor like she was a blushing bride being laid down on her bed. She opened her mouth to scream when she made that comparison, when she thought that she was about to be violated by this nightmare being that had somehow manifested in her home.

The fact that he was holding her gently and hushing her softly took a few minutes to sink in. He whispered all the way that he wasn't going to hurt her, wasn't even going to touch her. He just needed a little money and a change of clothes. He promised she'd be right as rain, she'd have a fun story to tell at church on Sunday. Everything would be alright. So long as she shut her damn mouth and stopped struggling.

She had not responded to the gentle words, but when that threat of violence arrived and his voice turned harsh, it was as though she transformed into the perfect pliant captive. She'd been given two choices, and she'd chosen the easy way out. He gave her a smile when she stopped wriggling. 'That's right. Everything's going to be right as rain. You just need to calm yourself.'

He was surprisingly careful with helping her back to her feet, even letting her go while he dug through the closet under the sink for some clothesline to tie her up with. 'Nothing to be scared of, just can't have you running around the place until I'm done. You got any cash in this place? Remember insurance will set you right. You won't really lose nothing.'

With rope in hand, he let her lead him through to the dining table she had set up in her living room. He settled her in one of the chairs and bent to tie her wrists, checking in with her to be sure that nothing was pinching. He was still playing through all of this as though he was the hero, escaping from unjust imprisonment. As if he hadn't stabbed a man over the price of a few beers. As if he wasn't every bit the monster that she had imagined him to be when she first set her eyes upon him.

Play-acting that he was still human, still decent—it made things easier for the both of them. He didn't have to do anything that he wasn't ready to do, and she didn't have to suffer through a bigger scare than being tied up and robbed in her own home by some smirking monster.

She eventually directed him to where she kept her purse, and he discovered the car keys inside it all on his own. With that taken care of, he turned back to her with that same smile that he truly believed was reassuring but which sent a chill down her spine. That smile made her tug against her bindings. It made her shake and close her eyes against the sight of him—which was why it took her by surprise when she felt him taking a grip on her head. Her eyes flew open. She thrashed. It didn't help. She couldn't escape him any more than she could escape gravity. Her strength was no match for his. He turned her to face him, and when she opened her mouth to scream, he stuffed a rag from under the sink into her mouth and wrapped more of the same rope around her face to hold it in place. 'Just need you to be quiet. I'm going to be gone for a couple minutes, and I don't need you getting any bright ideas about yelling for help while you're on your lonesome. Help will be coming in the morning, but for now, you need to behave yourself if you want this all to go nice and smoothly. You understand me?'

With a gag in her mouth and his hands still pinning her head in place, she had no means of agreeing, but he took that silence as assent, turning and leaving without another word to go hunt for some clothes.

There were more rooms than he would have guessed in the little house, and everywhere he turned there seemed to be more furniture to dig through. The place was oppressive, small but stuffed with all the memories that young folks would have been decent enough to throw away. Instead, he had to wade through them. Photo albums on top of coin collections on top of old makeup. Strata of a life long-lived. Some of it was worth something to somebody, but he'd be damned if he knew who could fence most of it. He needed quick and easy. The cash she had on hand would carry him a fair distance, but it wouldn't take him all the way.

In the master bedroom he hit the jackpot, a jewellery box full of old trinkets. Some of them had to be worth something, and jewellery was always the easiest stuff to pawn. If nothing else, he'd get the dollar's weight for the gold bits. Time was too tight to go digging through right now. He stuffed anything overhanging into the box and scooped up the whole thing. He needed clothes now that everything else was coming together. And since this bat had kept everything from her whole life, and he'd been pretty sure she had an old wedding ring on her finger, he was willing to bet that there were still boxes and boxes of her old dead hubby's clothes stowed away somewhere. He didn't mind if they were old and smelled like mothballs. He liked the classic fashions, and he'd drive with the windows down to air out the old people smell anyway.

The guest bedroom provided nothing in the way of clothes or valuables. Well, that wasn't strictly true—he'd dithered over some of her old collectables and things, fairly certain that they were worth a pretty penny, but once again, he had neither the knowledge nor the contacts to make good on them, so he let them be. No point in ripping the old girl's sentimental attachments apart if he wasn't even going to get cash for them. He wasn't a monster. He kept on telling himself that. Justifying to himself everything he was doing. He wasn't doing this because he was bad. He was on the run, fleeing an unjust sentence that had been passed down because all those folks from the bar had gotten together and decided to lie about how things had gone down. It wasn't because he enjoyed robbing old ladies and taking their things. Or because he got his rocks off by digging through yet another room full of dusty boxes to find himself a too-tight suit that looked like it hadn't seen the light of day since World War II.

He was doing this to survive. Nobody could begrudge him that. Even the old girl downstairs had understood that. She hadn't objected when he asked her for her things, hadn't struggled when he tied her up. Hell, she even took the gag like a champ.

He'd half expected to hear her muffled attempts at screaming through the gag as he went, but the house remained silent except for his rummaging and digging. He put her out of his mind. If she was willing to play ball, then he wasn't going to go bothering her.

At last, he managed to pull together something like a wearable outfit and slunk into the bathroom to get himself changed. He laughed to himself about it even as he still did it.

The politeness of stepping into a private room to change when there was no chance of anybody walking in on him anywhere. Not unless the husband was still around here somewhere, stuffed in one of the boxes or closets he hadn't gotten to yet.

He checked himself out in the mirror and found the view thoroughly acceptable, then he used the bathroom for its intended purpose before scooping up the jewellery, cash, and keys and heading towards the front door to make his escape. By his count, it was a little over an hour since he'd first arrived in the neighbourhood. Record time, considering the chaotic state the place had been in before he started ransacking it.

He was almost out the door before he felt another pang of conscience. The old lady. He could say goodbye to her at least, give her some reassurance. Make sure that she wasn't hurting. It wouldn't make up for robbing her, of course—he wasn't so deluded by his own lies that he believed she'd ever think of this as anything other than a terrible violation—but it helped to ease his own growing concern that he was a bad person, so he strolled back along the corridor with a spring in his step.

She was slumped forward against the restraints, and this time Paul did laugh out loud. Here he was worrying that she was uncomfortable, and she'd already fallen asleep in place. It was amazing, he'd barely been here any time at all, and she'd already gotten herself so comfortable that she'd passed right out.

He went down onto his haunches beside her, so he could look at her one last time before heading out. That was when he saw the greenish-yellow dribbling from around the edges of her gag.

'What?'

He took hold of her by the shoulders and gave her a shake. When she didn't stir, he tried again, before resorting to a slap in the face when she still wouldn't wake up. The slap loosened up the gag enough that some of the vomit managed to escape, slithering out past the gag to run down her front, filling the room with its acrid stench.

Paul fell over backwards, scrambling away from her in a crab walk. She was dead. He'd done nothing wrong. He'd done everything, same as last time. Why would she be dead? It made no sense. He hadn't done anything to her. Why was she dead?

When he hit the wall, he slumped down, sitting there and staring at the dead woman, trying to piece together how this could have happened. How everything could have gone so wrong when he had done everything right.

It wasn't fair. None of this was fair. He didn't deserve to be in jail for a million years, just because his body had done something he hadn't told it to do. He didn't deserve to be facing a murder charge now. And he knew that he would have to face that if they caught him. There was no way that they'd look at this situation and see the accident in it. There was no way that the benefit of the doubt would be extended his way. It never had been, and it never would be. Even if some clever coroner looked at the old bag's body and worked out how she'd died, they'd still blame it on him. He'd been the one to tie her up and gag her, so if she died while she was tied up and gagged, it was his fault. Everything was always his fault.

He was turning over a new leaf, he was going to get himself organised and plan for the future, and now it was all coming apart at the seams before it had even begun.

It wasn't fair. So he wasn't going to let it ruin his life. He always told himself he'd take his lumps when he'd earned them. God knew he'd gone willingly back to his father every time he'd done something wrong knowing exactly what kind of bloody vengeance was going to be enacted on him. But he hadn't earned a life sentence for robbing some old lady's house. She wasn't even meant to be here today. It was just godawful luck.

He shouldn't have to pay for bad luck. That wasn't justice. It wasn't right. He was trying to do the right thing. Get a car, get out of town, keep his head down. But this stupid old woman had to go and die on him for no reason at all. He wasn't paying for it. He wasn't.

So he did what he had promised himself that he would do while lying in his cell. He started planning ahead. He had cash, clothes, and a car: all the pieces that would get him out of reach of the police dragnet. All that he needed to do was keep moving. Cleaning up here, he was just going to make more of a mess for himself. He didn't know the first thing about hiding bodies, and he was on a deadline that would not shift regardless of how well he covered up his crimes. Haste mattered more than cleanliness right about now. So he did the only thing that he could do. He walked right past the dead old woman still tied to her chair, out the front door, and drove away.

He'd left his prints all over the house. He had motive coming out of his ass. He'd left no shortage of clues that it was him who had committed the crime, but there was still hope for him.

The machinery of justice was slow turning, and each little cog spun for a while before it connected up with the next. If he was over the state line before his name and that dead old girl could be clipped together, then he could slip through the cracks just like he and so many of his cellmates through the years had managed to do.

That was the funny thing about prison—it hadn't made him into a better man, but it had turned him into a far better criminal. One who could see all the holes woven into the fabric of society. One who could step right through those holes to emerge unscathed on the other side. He'd never been the most sociable of prisoners, but he'd always been a good listener. Quick to learn. When the crooks and the killers had been talking, his ears had been wide open, learning the tricks of the trade for the next time that he was set loose.

All he had to do was keep on moving and everything would work out just fine. Yeah, when somebody finally found the body, there would be suspicions that he was involved in the old girl's death, but they'd have to send out forensics, and they'd have to take samples, and they'd have to run tests on the samples, and they'd need paperwork written up and signed and notarized.

Everything moved at a crawl on the other side of the law. They'd need a warrant for his arrest signed before they could even touch him for this, and if he got his old lawyer back in the game, there were decent odds that that genius in a suit could sniff out some mistakes that they'd made and put a hole in their boat before it even took sail.

So the plan, such as it was, remained unchanged. Nobody had seen him come in here, nobody was going to help the cops join the dots any quicker. All he had to do was roll out of town without anybody that knew him seeing him and high tail it over the border to Georgia. Then from Atlanta he had the whole of the south open to him.

It didn't feel right. It felt disrespectful, somehow, for an old lady to be dead and for it not to change anything. He should have had to jump through some extra hoops. Somebody dying should have meant something. But it didn't. Paul rolled out of her driveway without it changing a damn thing. He couldn't even bring himself to feel sorry for her. He was sorry that she was dead, but only because of the trouble it was going to cause him, not because a life had suddenly and wrongly been snuffed out. It had been an accident, and normally an accidental death would have at least made him feel a twinge of pity, but today all he had was annoyance.

She could have died any other night, but she chose this one. She was old, any minute could have been her last, but she decided to drop dead in the one minute when it could be blamed on him.

It was hard to tell whether the engine or Paul was growling louder by the time he started the car up and swerved out into the street. Frustration clawed at his throat as he tried to maintain his focus. Stick to the plan. Get out of Dodge. Think things through.

It had always been the stupid mistakes that got him caught. The loose ends he'd never tied off. Well, this time he was prepared, with his metaphorical scissors at the ready. As he headed off towards his mother's house, and the stash of his old belongings that he had secreted around the neighbourhood, his eyes were in constant motion.

There was nobody around but him and the floral reek of the old girl's perfume still lingering in the car. No pedestrians, no other drivers, but still his gaze flickered about the place, searching for the first sign of trouble. The ominous flash of blue and red. The howl of the siren.

It didn't feel right. Getting away with murder. Even if he knew he wasn't really responsible, even if he knew that he didn't deserve to get caught, it still felt like there was a disruption in the natural order of things. He'd always clung to the idea that none of the laws and rules that people laid down for themselves were necessary. That they were self-imposed prisons that crushed the spirit and the mind until everybody all behaved exactly the same, ignoring what really mattered to them so that they could chase after somebody else's American dream. Yet now, here he was, internally lamenting the idea that none of it really mattered.

It was all her fault. Not the dead old woman. Angela. She'd been the one to get him all turned around and mixed up. Promising him all the stuff he'd seen in the movies that didn't exist out here in the real world. It was a cruel trick that she'd played on him, making him believe. Giving him hope. He'd thrown away everything that he'd ever believed in for her, for her promise of a better world, where the good and the righteous were rewarded instead of taken advantage of. He'd bought it hook, line, and sinker. All the lies he'd spent his life running from. She was the one at fault here, really. If it hadn't been for her, he never would have been mad enough to stab somebody. If it hadn't been for her, he would have quietly served out his sentence in silence then gotten back to doing what he'd always done without a moment's delay. It was all her fault. Everything that had happened was because she had messed his head up.

Everything that he did was because of her. Everything he would do was because of her. No matter how hard he tried to escape from the memory of the love he'd felt, he couldn't.

Falling Dominos

The neighbourhood where his mother lived was still dead silent as dawn approached. On his way over, there had been the first few cars and pedestrians of the day rolling around, but nobody looked at him twice. It wasn't like he was roaring about the place at top speed. Even though his hind-brain was begging him to get the hell out of town as fast as possible, slow and steady was the course that would keep him under the radar. This was the difference between the old Paul and the new. He was thinking now. He was keeping his instincts under control. It didn't matter that he could reach for a gun and pluck it out of a cop's holster, it didn't matter that he could draw a knife and plunge it into somebody's liver, it didn't matter that he could put his foot down on the accelerator and be all the way out of Florida by nightfall. He was still capable of all those things, but now they were only going to happen when he decided to make them happen. He was not going to become a murderer by accident. Not again. He was in control of himself. His rational, planning mind was what was going to save him, not his body's hardwired responses.

So he drove to his mother's house, left the car by the roadside, scampered into the garden to retrieve his bag from where he'd stowed it away, and then returned to the street at the same calm and steady pace at which he had been doing everything since the old lady died.

More time had given him more opportunity to think. The car he was in would be connected to a murder. All he had to do was switch to another one, dump this one somewhere, and the connection with him might never be made. Fingerprints could do it, but the cops only fell back on that sort of technology when they had to. There were sure to be some locals that they'd like for the crime, somebody to bear the blame so that he could slow his pace. That was the other thing that he'd realised—the dragnet to catch him would only last a day or two at best, set up on the motorways out of town. After that, they'd assume he'd already slipped by them. If he could be smart about this, take his time, distance himself from the accidental death, he could just hop into somebody else's car and be on his merry way without a backwards glance. He was so used to letting his gut run the show that, now his mind was in charge, he couldn't help but feel a little sheepish about what a fool he'd acted all his life.

Step one was dumping the car. Somewhere in this neighbourhood might be too clear a connection to his mother, and therefore him, but too much time driving around exacerbated the risk. A nearby neighbourhood then, one that could easily be driven to from the dead old woman's house if you were hauling away stolen goods but didn't want the hassle of a hot car. Cops loved a good story, if you fed them a nice easy one, they'd keep on chasing it long after the truth had left town.

With his newly retrieved duffel, he reshuffled things to be more mobile: stowed the cash away at the bottom, put some of his own clothes on, tucked a revolver into the waistline of his jeans. Then he was on his merry way once more, setting off at the same leisurely pace as before. No rush to go anywhere, nothing exciting about him. Just some stranger rolling around in his car on a bright and beautiful morning.

So long as he remained a stranger, there was no problem. It was only when he was perceived that trouble might arise.

It was around this time that several events were happening concurrently. Paul's escape from the cells had been noticed, and a manhunt was lumbering slowly into action—although even by the rather lax standards of the time, it was slow moving, with many outright disbelieving that Paul had successfully escaped, preferring to believe that he had simply been transferred elsewhere and the paperwork was causing the problem. He didn't strike anyone as a master criminal, and none of his recorded actions led them to believe that he was capable of arranging with outside forces to secure his freedom. The idea that a prisoner could simply pick locks and walk themselves out of jail didn't cross anyone's mind. It was a stupid man's solution to a complex problem. Blunt force applied to a situation that most would approach with a desire for surgical precision to avoid detection. By the time he was dumping the car that would connect him to a completely different crime, they still hadn't started looking for him.

Simultaneously, other events were unfolding. Alice Curtis's son came to visit and discovered her dead body, still tied to the chair. Having no idea that he was about to contaminate a crime scene, he rushed in to free her from her bonds, not even understanding that she was already dead. With her loose from her restraints, he finally recognised that she was not breathing. With his thoughts only for her, he immediately called an ambulance and began working to try and revive her, wiping the dried sick from around her mouth and desperately attempting to breathe life back into a body that had long since turned cold. He went on like that until the paramedics arrived, and it was only after they had done all that they could and declared her dead that the police were finally informed of the situation.

As it turned out, Curtis had died because she wore dentures. With the gag tied tightly about her head, they had been forced out of place, the back plate pushing into her throat, where she had inevitably begun gagging on them before vomiting and choking. It was pure bad luck that she had slipped them back into her mouth before investigating the odd sounds downstairs. If any of a dozen different things had happened just a little differently, then she would have survived her brush with Paul Knowles, and none of the events that followed would have become 'necessary.'

With that cause of death established, the police began treating the case less like an accidental death and more like the manslaughter that it was. Forensic teams swept the house for any evidence of her killer, but after the ambulance staff and her son's intervention, there was too much contamination for them to ascertain who was responsible. The absence of any fingerprints suggested to them that they were dealing with a burglary gone wrong, committed by a consummate professional.

This was exactly the opposite of any profile that they might have constructed around Paul Knowles, who was still treated like an incompetent, blundering his way through life and causing problems for himself. Worse yet, the connection could not be made with Knowles at all. Because the time of his escape from imprisonment was completely unknown, there was a huge window of opportunity in which he might have made his escape. His imprisonment might very well have provided him with an alibi for the crime, and given that everything else about the crime in question was unlike his priors and that the system wasn't even ready to acknowledge that he was free at that time, he had slipped through the cracks entirely unnoticed. It was all that he could have hoped for and more. All that he needed to do was get a new car and drive out of town and he'd be free.

Lillian and Mylette Anderson were neighbours of his mother. More specifically, they were the children of one of her neighbours. Lillian was eleven and took her job as caretaker for seven-year-old Mylette very seriously when they were out playing together, rarely taking her eyes off her. They were a common sight around town, playing together and with all of their friends. What had brought them streets away from home into a whole other neighbourhood so early in the day remains unknown. They'd always been prone to wandering, and the town was considered safe enough that nobody would give the little girls a second look as they went by. Kids played outside in the 70s; that was the normal state of affairs.

Paul drove right past them. They never looked his way. They probably wouldn't have recognised either him or the car, but he recognised them. He knew them, and he knew that if they had seen him, it would connect him to the car and back to the dead lady he'd left behind. They were now one of the loose ends that his new enlightened lifestyle could not tolerate. All it would take was them mentioning to their mother that they'd seen him in town, recalling the colour of the car, or the make, any little detail would have been enough to connect the dots when the cops did finally come around to ask his family and their neighbours questions.

It was a mark of how much he had changed, and how rapidly, that he proceeded calmly along with his original plan, dumping the stolen car, proceeding on foot for several blocks before identifying a new one, and then quietly breaking in, hotwiring it and moving on. At this point, his original plan was to exit town in an unusual direction, head out into the country and travel by lesser-known roads off the beaten track to circle his way around and head for the state border. However, circumstances had changed, and he was adapting to them as he went, his plans evolving to suit what was happening around him instead of him trying to force his way ahead despite fresh resistance.

Turning back from the road straight out of town, he drove back along the streets he had just walked, back to the car he had dumped, and then past it towards where he had spotted the girls in play. They had moved on from that spot by the time that he arrived, but he did not let that concern him. There was a limited distance that little girls could walk in the time that they'd had. He just had to do like the police did when they tried to catch up to him: set a perimeter and work out towards it. If those dumb cops could pull it off, there was no way that he couldn't work it out.

Keeping his pace slow and steady, he slid silently along one residential street after another. Nobody knew him here, there was nothing to fear. All he had to worry about was keeping his eyes open. If he had to head back towards his mother's place, then the risk might outweigh the benefit of catching up to them. A few more witnesses and the whole thing would spiral out of control and he'd need to cut his losses. Even if the new car disconnected him from the old lady's murder, he didn't need too many people knowing his whereabouts for when the cops came knocking about the whole prison break thing.

He need not have worried. The girls had not been moving at maximum speed trying to avoid capture, so just a few blocks over from where he'd last seen them, they were dithering in the shade of some trees, playing some game, sing-songing back and forth. It was almost too easy.

They did recognise him this time around—they knew him as the son of their neighbour, a vaguely friendly adult face that sometimes passed by on the periphery of their lives. So when he told them that their parents were worried sick looking for them, and that he was to take them home right away, they believed him. After all, this wasn't some kind of stranger like they'd been warned to stay away from. This was Paul from next door, and they were far more afraid of their parent's wrath than of him. They practically leapt into the back seat of the car on hearing that they were in trouble, arguing with each other about whether or not their mother had heard them telling her they were going out for the morning. Quietly cursing that nobody ever listened to them.

They were so intent on their own internal drama, and so young and unfamiliar with the world outside of their little corner of suburbia, that they did not even notice that they were heading in entirely the wrong direction. Even as minutes of driving turned to nigh on an hour, they didn't question it. Time is supremely malleable to children, stretching out and tightening up when they aren't looking. Hours of play could feel like minutes, and moments of dread of coming punishment and arguments could stretch out into hours. It was only when they finally looked outside of the window and realised that town was far behind them that they began to fear, but even still, they had been raised to be respectful of their elders, so it took them far longer than it should have to question their driver as to where they were going.

He lied to them of course, said that their parents had gone out to visit somebody in the sticks—that's why they'd sent him instead of coming for the girls themselves. He was meant to bring them out there. As if that were a completely normal thing, as if any parent would leave town without their children. As if this whole thing wasn't mad.

If he was being honest, Paul didn't expect them to believe him, dumb as he truly thought kids were, but at this point, it wasn't as though they had any choice but to stay put by now. This was long before the days of mobile phones. If they were dumped out of the car way out here in the middle of nowhere, they'd have no way of getting back to town, back to safety. Even if they did try to fight him for control of the car, he was pretty sure he could take them. Even if he somehow couldn't, it wasn't as though they could drive the car. They were utterly defenceless. Had been from the start. It was only now that they started to realise it and start to worry about what that meant for their immediate future. Neither had been old enough to learn about the truly awful things that could happen out in the wilds of the world to a little girl. The dangers they'd imagined and prepared against were things like stray dogs, getting lost, and crossing busy roads. They were innocent, and it had damned them.

Out in the middle of some godforsaken swamp so far from civilisation that they couldn't even see another human being, he finally stopped the car. Lillian was the only one to muster up the courage to speak by then. Asking why they'd stopped, why they'd stopped here in the middle of nowhere, where their parents were. Maybe that was why when he got out of the car, he went around to her side first.

All that little Mylette could do was watch as her sister was pinned down to the seat beside her, with the monstrous bulk of a full-grown man looming over, hands locked around her big sister's throat. She screamed of course, but out there in the middle of the bayou there was nobody around to hear it but the mosquitos. She even tried slapping at the man's hands, trying to pull him off her sister, but there was no way that a child could dislodge the full weight of a grown man bearing down.

Paul's weight more than his strength was the determining factor in the struggle with Lillian. He didn't have to do much more than put his hands into the right place and then lean to crush her airway. The squeezing that he did at the sides was superfluous when his weight had crushed her larynx. Still, he stayed there on top of her, with her little sister screaming and flailing, until finally he was satisfied that she would never move again.

That was when he looked up to Mylette.

It was only in that moment that she seemed to grasp the mortal danger that she was in, that a man who had murdered her only and best protector in the world was now staring at her with the same blank expression that had been on his face throughout the slaughter that she had just witnessed. She was going to die. It was an alien thought for someone so young. Never in her seven years of life had she ever encountered a situation like this. Never had she needed to entertain the thought of it. Her sister had worried for her, watched for cars coming, held her hand when they crossed the road, but she had never needed to think about the why. She had humoured all of her sister's insistent worries, of course, but they'd never felt real.

This felt real. The cramped heat of the car, the glass of the window against the back of her head as her feet slipped over the leather seat covers. This all felt far too real to be the nightmare that she had clearly fallen into. Twisting and kicking her legs like she was already being strangled, she managed to grab hold of the door handle and pushed her way out to freedom. Paul stopped crawling over the back seat, and the dead girl, to step back out of the car, too.

Mylette ran as though her life depended on it. Never once looking back, never once letting the tears streaming down her face slow her. But it didn't matter. Out here in the swamp, the ground was soft, and her legs were too short. If she'd made it free of Paul, there would have been snakes, gators, and worse waiting for her out there. It was almost a blessing that she barely made it off the road before he caught her.

This time there was no lucky angle that would let weight do the work. This time Paul had to squeeze with all of his might, thumbs digging into the soft skin beneath her chin, hands so tight they felt like they might cramp as they crushed the neck beneath. She was too short, so there was strain, first on his back as he hunched over to choke her, then on his arms as he straightened up and lifted her whole body off the ground by the throat. Gravity helped out a little from then on, but she didn't have nearly enough weight to make it an easy kill.

If there was any justice in the world, it would have been quick, but the fact that she was so tiny rendered the long process of her death all the more arduous. She dangled and she wriggled and she tried to scream for help even though there was nothing in her lungs but burning. She wept and she flailed. Any other man would have faltered in the face of it. The man that Paul had been just a week before would have faltered in the face of it. But he had changed. The world had made itself his enemy, and he could no longer afford to trust in luck. That meant thinking things through and then doing whatever was necessary to ensure his continued survival and freedom. He looked that little girl dead in the eyes as he choked the life from her tiny body, and when he was sure she was dead and turning cold in his grip, only then did he let himself feel some measure of grief. Not for her, never for her, but for himself. For having been reduced to murdering children just to get along. He cursed the world for making things this way. Cursed the law for doing him wrong. Cursed everyone except the one who had just damned himself.

With both girls dead, he carried them off out into the swamp, one at a time, picking a random direction, and threw them into the brackish water, not even bothering to see if they'd sink before heading back to his car and heading off. Not north, where everyone would have been expecting him to go, where he would have gone just a day before, but to the east, out towards the coast.

The Road to Ruin

Nowadays, Atlantic Beach is considered to be essentially a part of the town of Jacksonville, but back in the 70s, there was some space between them. A little breathing room between a faltering seaside resort and the population that used it on the weekends. The population out there was small, and they got all the benefits of tourism with a nice lull through the week that made it into essentially a small, peaceful coastal village. The kind of place where you wouldn't think twice about leaving the door unlocked or inviting a stranger to dinner. An innocent place, where the worst thing that happened was pickpockets coming in from the big city at the weekend to prey on tourists.

When Paul arrived, fresh from the scene of a double murder, he didn't raise a single eyebrow.

He knew that moving on fast would be the expectation of anyone hunting him, so he took things easy, drew no attention to himself. Spent a little bit of money on a proper place to sleep, ate a few meals in the local diner. He needed a little bit of time to think, and he figured that hiding right under the noses of the police was the best way to get that time. By now, his escape was public knowledge, but apart from being a minor embarrassment for law enforcement, nobody outside of government was giving him much of a thought. He'd been on the news once or twice, an old headshot from an earlier arrest, but ultimately the public weren't exactly living in fear of a man guilty of assaulting somebody in a bar fight. He barely lasted a news cycle before fading back into obscurity.

The missing girls garnered considerably more media attention, particularly in the local communities, where people were asked to be on the lookout for them. There was no suspicion that they were runaways, but they were both very young, and it was quite possible that they had become lost or climbed onto the wrong bus and ended up somewhere unfamiliar. Just as nobody thought that the girls had deliberately fled, nobody was talking about their disappearance in terms of abduction either. As for the death of Alice Curtis, it did the same brief rounds in the news at about the same time, but nobody was connecting any dots.

Still, Paul did not let down his guard. He did not act out, or even have more than a couple of beers in the evening. Not after the last time he had been properly roaring drunk and lost all control over himself. That could never happen again. He needed to remain in control if he was going to stay free. It was a funny little dichotomy of thought that he struggled to wrap his head around. He had to enforce rules on himself so that he didn't have to live with the rules of others. It was almost like his whole failed attempt at romance, where he was willing to accept some restrictions on his freedoms so that he could get the thing that he wanted more. For all his obsession with freedom, he was becoming his own jailer. His own taskmaster. His own father.

This, more than the idea that he had slaughtered two children, was haunting him, keeping him up at night and filling his waking hours with confusion. Every time that he thought he'd made a plan for what to do next, he found himself tearing it down again. Every time that he thought that he'd gotten the matter settled with himself, it would rear its ugly head once more.

Eventually, Paul settled upon one of his usual solutions to the more complex psychological problems that he encountered in his life: hedonism. He would follow the rules that he was laying out for himself, ensuring that he was in complete control at all times, and he would also reward himself wildly for every little encroachment on his freedom so that it did not feel so much like a punishment. His only experience with anything resembling work in his life had been in prison camps and chain gangs. The idea of putting effort into doing something that he did not want to do in exchange for a payoff at the end had never really entered into his understanding of the world. So, what he now considered a revolutionary change within himself was essentially the simple compromise that every adult living in society has to make. To endure that which is not immediately pleasurable so that greater pleasure can be achieved further down the line. It bears repeating at this juncture that Paul was not in fact a stupid man, to find such simple concepts so baffling, but he was someone who had grown up outside the regular construct of society. So many of its inner workings were as alien to him as the thrumming of an active beehive would be to you or me.

With the philosophical debate on free will and self-discipline resolved, Paul was ready to move on again. His pursuers would have grossly overshot him by now, looking in every direction other than their own doorsteps, and he was finally settled enough within himself that he felt like he could proceed without tripping over his own confused thoughts. The only minor hitch was that the limited supply of money he'd acquired through the burglary immediately after his breakout was dwindling after this pleasant little holiday from his usual life, and with his intention to stay put and draw no attention to himself, he could hardly be topping it off with his usual housebreaking.

It wouldn't be a problem. Really. He'd already been staking out houses around town as a matter of course, and there was no shortage of pawn shops in any small town. He'd already used a couple to dispose of the remnants from his last break-in.

There was no fear of failure or capture in him, only that nagging memory of his last burglary gone so wrong and what could have happened to him as a result. That old woman had seen his face, he'd chatted with her. It wouldn't have taken the cops two seconds to put together her description and their escaped convict. He'd been so stupid. Every time he felt he'd carefully thought things through, he just proved himself even more of an idiot. Things weren't the same anymore. Getting arrested wouldn't be a slap on the wrist. He wouldn't bounce back out of jail in a month or two. If he wanted to stay free, then he was going to have to pay the price for that freedom.

Or, more accurately, Marjorie Howie was going to pay the price for his freedom.

As his ability to plan developed, the way that he committed his crimes evolved too. More often than not, when he had been arrested for burglary in the past it was because he had been spotted during the breaking and entering portion of the evening. If he could eliminate the need for that, then he could eliminate the risk. Once he was inside a house, he was basically invisible to the outside world, so all that he needed was a way to enter the home without it looking suspicious to passers-by.

It required a rethink of the approach to his crimes from the ground up, but since his arrival at Atlantic Beach, all that Paul had was time to think, and while he'd suffered utter humiliation when his fiancée rejected him and sent him away, that did not mean that he had learned no lessons in romance and seduction over the course of their correspondence. He'd always had considerable success with the ladies—there is always something appealing about a bad boy, but he had never considered that aspect of his life and his criminal 'job' to be related to one another. It had never occurred to him that the skills he used to trick girls into his bed could have other applications.

In the end, he did not go to any of the houses that he had staked out because, instead, he let his prey come to him.

Avoiding the usual dive bars that he preferred, Paul spent a couple of nights migrating around the more upscale places in town. Nowhere too expensive, where he'd stand out like a sore thumb, but nowhere with sawdust on the floor either. Strangely, for him, he was barely drinking either—nursing a couple of beers through the night even though he had enough cash in his pocket to be drinking whiskey. The goal wasn't to get drunk, or even to have a good time. The goal was to eye up the crowd, wait for a weak one to break off from the herd. Or rather the complete opposite. All night long, the crowd gradually dwindled as the more attractive of the drinkers paired off and headed out for some debauchery. There were a few times that it looked like there was interest in Paul, if only for the novelty of a fresh face in a tired scene, but he fobbed them off quickly before anyone could really grasp that was what was happening. It was too early in the night, and he needed someone different. His goal wasn't to find the hottest, youngest thing; it was to find the right kind of lady. The kind with the right sort of assets.

It was coming up on closing time when he narrowed in on the one that he wanted. Marjorie Howie was 49, right on the upper end of the age bracket for the barfly crowd and struggling to make any headway with the single men her own age. When Paul started talking with her, she may have mistaken it for pity rather than interest, then when he started coming onto her, she was probably more confused than interested. It took him as long to convince her that he actually wanted her as to convince her that she wanted him—although that second task was markedly easier, given that he was young, gorgeous, and clearly offering himself up on a silver platter. Turned out he was a visitor in town, so he didn't have any place to take her other than his hotel room on the other side of town, and going there would be tantamount to admitting that they had no intention of 'carrying on the conversation'. She wasn't desperate enough to commit to that. She had a little bit of decorum. He could come back to her house for a nightcap, and if she decided there that she still wanted to take him to bed then it would be a private matter that nobody in town would need to know about. Her house was just a few blocks away anyway. Maybe the cool night air would help clear her head. She was dizzy from the drink and flushed from the excitement. Cool heads won out, so she had to cool hers right down as soon as possible.

It seemed that this young gentleman was not willing or able to keep his hands to himself that long. The moment they were away from the light of the bar he was kissing her, his big hands running up and down her arms, reminding her of all the things she'd been missing for far too long.

Her head did not clear by the time they were fumbling with the handle of her front door. She barely even remembered walking the distance from the bar. In fact, she was half convinced that he'd carried her a portion of the way, with the way that his hands were locked on the back of her thighs, sliding up under the hem of her skirt. Rucking up her nylons. They got inside and she had to kick the door shut. Her hands were too busy fiddling with the buttons of his shirt. Why did they have to make them so small and fiddly when she needed to be touching his bare skin right now? His own hands had stopped groping all over her now. She heard the lock click shut. Thank God one of them had some sense left in them.

There was no way they were going to make it to the bedroom, not with the speed at which the whole world felt like it was coming apart at the seams. All she knew was heat and passion. His hands up under her hemline, pulling her nylons down as she fumbled to toe off her shoes. Her breath was coming harsh against his lips in those moments that she drew away to catch some air, but he did not seem to be struggling at all. It must have been youth giving him vigour. She couldn't wait to see how that would translate into the rest of their evening. In the living room, the bared backs of her legs hit the arm of the sofa and she tipped over backwards, torn away from Paul for just a moment. He stood there, looking down at her, still and calm. She could hardly believe it. That little smirk, still fixed on his lips beneath her smeared lipstick. He knew exactly what he was doing to her, and he was enjoying it. With almost painful slowness, he ran his fingers down the length of her legs, hooking them onto her tights and pulling them down the rest of the way until they were left dangling from his fingertips and she was exposed to him.

His eyes travelled back the way that his hands had gone, trailing oh-so-slowly all the way up the length of her legs, her body, to her face. She could feel the heat of that stare. The weight of it, brushing over her. When they locked eyes, she felt like she was frozen in place, like a gazelle caught alone by a lion. Her whole body shook with anticipation.

He pounced.

In an instant, he went from standing there to being on top of her, in an instant her anticipation was tipped over the edge into the moment that it was all going to happen. She thrust her hands down, struggling to undo his belt as he pressed his lips to hers. Fighting to move her arms at all as the weight of his body pinned them between their bodies. She had lost all control of the situation and she didn't even care. Let him take control. Let him do whatever he wanted. Nothing she could think of could be better than this. Nothing she wanted could be better than what he was going to do to her of his own volition, unprompted.

Anticipation came burning up through her again. His hands were on either side of her head. He was pushing himself up, and away from her. The stupid nylons still tangled on his hands. She tried to reach up and drag them free, but for all that he'd drawn his body up to look down on her, her hands were still thoroughly trapped in between their bodies. The stupid tights were pressing on her chin, strung between his hands, and while she laughed, it was uncomfortable. He reared back a little, giving her space to move, but then the moment that she lifted her head up, he did something, twisting his hands around, tangling the nylons beneath her head.

He'd seemed so slick back in the bar, but now she could see that with youth she was going to have to deal with clumsiness. She gave him a smile to assure him that this was all going to be a funny story later, not anything to get embarrassed or upset about, but when she met his eyes, a new chill ran through her body that had nothing to do with the heat between them. When she looked into his eyes, they looked dead. The man who had been lusting after her, chasing after her—he was gone. And replacing him there was an expressionless mannequin. Eyes dead and dark, like a shark's.

She opened her mouth to speak, to scream maybe, but she found no sound coming out. That was when she finally felt the burning. The nylons had been looped around her neck, and now Paul was pulling them tight, hauling on them with all his strength, while his body still pinned her down. She tried to pull herself free of him or push him off, but she'd already been breathless before the noose of underwear tightened around her throat, and now her lungs burned. Strength fled her as swiftly as her excitement and arousal. If this was some sort of game, she didn't want to play. He was scaring her. The dead expression leering down at her told her all too clearly that it was not a game, but she was still clinging to some false hope that this might just be a misunderstanding about what the two of them wanted in the bedroom.

For his part, Paul was already growing bored waiting for her to die. He began to look around the room for anything that would be worthwhile stealing once she was dead.

This was how all of his burglaries would be committed going forward. This was the logical way to eliminate any evidence that the prior owners of his ill-gotten gains might have provided to the police. He was making it so that he left no trail behind him. He hadn't even brought a weapon to the scene of this fresh crime, fully intending to do the deed with his bare hands, as he had with the little girls, before realising just how much easier things could be with a little garotte strung between his hands.

The television was definitely going to be worth something. None of the ornaments looked fancy enough to get more than a couple of bucks for them. In the bedroom there'd be jewellery. God knows Marjorie was wearing enough of it. Like enough sparkling things around her sagging face might distract anybody from just how old and unattractive she was becoming. He'd strip that off her body when he took her clothes and burn them to eliminate any traces of himself. Even if it wasn't all real gold, there was always resale value in it.

When he glanced back down at her, that gold shone all the brighter against the purple of her skin. Blood was trickling out around where the nylon had bitten into her neck, and beneath that line of demarcation, she still looked as normal as when he'd picked her up. Her necklaces still lay on human-coloured flesh, even if there were some wrinkles he didn't like to see amidst her cleavage. Both alive and dead depending on where his eyes turned.

Somewhere in the midst of the struggle she had lost consciousness, but he hadn't noticed. His mind had already moved on from his point of entry into the building, into the best way to search it, strip it of all its goods, and then get out. Yet despite all of his attention being elsewhere, his body still obeyed the last command that he had given it. Even as his hands ached from where the twisted nylon was biting into them, he did not loosen his grip, through all the dreadful minutes he remained perfectly still.

Finally, he decided that the woman was dead, released his grip, and gave her one final glance for confirmation. Even though he had only chosen her for the air of money about her, she had been pretty enough. It hadn't really been any great imposition for him to kiss her, to hold her, to want her the way that she so obviously needed him to. Truth be told, if it hadn't been for his more pressing need for money than companionship, it isn't impossible he would have picked her anyway. She might not have been the prettiest thing in the bar that night, but he was certain they would have had a great time together. Now she barely even looked human anymore. Her head was swollen, all of her features bloated and twisted beyond recognition, discoloured past the puce of his original choking into some awful dark purple, turning to black in places. If he hadn't known what she looked like before, then there was no way he would recognise her now.

Sometime in the struggle, she'd managed to get her arms free. She'd reached up past the end of the sofa and caught hold of the telephone, dragging the handle off the base, and leaving the pulsing dial tone the only sound in the whole house now that Paul's grunts of effort were at an end. She'd pulled so hard on it that the wire had come unpinned from the wall, as if even in her final throes, with her throat crushed beyond all recognition, she was trying to call out for help. Paul disentangled himself from the corpse and put the mouthpiece back where it belonged, silencing the electronic thrumming. Nobody had heard that. There was no operator listening in, trying to decipher the meaning of the soft grunts of effort that he'd been letting out. This was not the good old days where there was someone just waiting on the end of the line. The switchboard was automatic now. Whatever hope she might have had, it had been foolish.

He chuckled at the thought of her final moments, thinking she was actually doing something to save herself. He looked down at her. It was almost a pity that he was going to be leaving the body behind. If this were one for dumping, he probably could have left it on the steps up to a police station and nobody would have been able to identify her for days, or even weeks. He might have made her a Jane Doe if he didn't have a plan that he was already sticking to. As it was, he was certain nobody from the bar was going to remember his meeting with her, and even if they somehow did manage to tie his description to the dead woman, it wasn't as though anybody would think to look for Paul here.

Stripping the apartment of anything of value was easy. There was none of the chaos from his last victim's house. Everything was in its place, easy to find, no secrets squirrelled away and no need to go digging for more. Not when that big expensive television was sitting right there, six feet from her cooling body, and all of her other worldly possessions carefully unpacked as though she had only just moved into the place and hadn't yet started living there. None of the gradual build-up of miscellanea, none of the forgetful misplacing. Everything was where it should be, so everything was his for the taking. It was one of the best hauls of his entire career as a burglar. He calculated enough money coming from this one night's work that he probably wouldn't need to rob again for weeks if he didn't want to. He'd be able to do exactly as he had planned from the beginning: cross the border, keep his head down, live easy for a while until he was certain that the hunt for him hadn't spread that far, and then set out on the road again with his whole life leading away like that asphalt into the distance.

Warmth spread through him that had nothing to do with the buzz he'd felt killing or the other heat he'd felt in the run-up, when he was putting his moves on her. Surprisingly, it was contentment. All of the suffering that he'd put himself through these last few days, with self-control and discipline and all of the other little prisons he'd always loathed, they'd all paid off. This was the reward for a little bit of self-denial. This was the reward for the new path that he'd set himself on. He hadn't even had to step out of line to reward himself. It had come to him. All the money he could spend, all for the small price of denying himself instant gratification every moment of the day. He could live with this. He could thrive like this.

The true cost of his newfound wealth lay perfectly still on the sofa, cooling slowly to room temperature, as he heaped up everything of value beside her. He then slunk out to go fetch his car from where he'd left it by the bar. Marjorie Howie had not deserved a fate like this. She had not been a bad person, or even one particularly inclined to the kind of nightlife that might have left her exposed to men like Paul Knowles. Just this one night, her loneliness had overwhelmed her, and she had gone out looking for some sort of human connection. Estranged recently from her husband, she had been trying to start over in this little place. Her kids were all grown up, and she no longer needed to hold everything together for their sake. She was taken with a need to recreate herself from the ground up, in some degree of isolation.

Who she was before this desire took her was already someone worthy of affection—a member of Saint John's Catholic Church and a proud part of the American Association of University Women. By any measure, she had lived a successful life, achieving things that the women of a generation ago could never have come close to. Educated, employed, and married for most of her adult life with grown children and grandchildren, to boot. Everything that she should have wanted, she'd had, but she'd craved something more. Some sort of passion or love beyond the barely dutiful attention that her husband had paid her. She deserved more. She deserved better.

But in the end, this was the price that she had paid for wanting to be loved.

It wasn't even as if there had been a gamble involved, where she knew that something like this might happen to her. It was 1974, and the horror stories of serial killers skulking in the shadows had not reached the ears of the average person. Even if Marjorie had known of them, it would have been in an abstract way. The kind of nightmare monsters who went after prostitutes in the big cities of the world. Not normal people like her. She had lived twenty years and more in this quiet town, this little bastion of peace in an ever more chaotic world. She'd made it through all the little challenges that life had thrown at her and never once flinched. She had lived through a world war without ever tasting violence. And now she was dead, simply because one man had decided that her television and the jewellery that she wore when she went to a bar were worth more to him than having another human being alive.

Everything that she had been, and everything that she might have become, was destroyed by his selfish desire for money.

Before the next day had even begun to break, Paul was back on the road again, heading up the coast towards Georgia and all of the fresh opportunities that it offered up to him. Nobody would know him there. The police would not be looking for him anymore. Any dangling threads from the crime scenes he'd left behind would be neatly snipped off the moment that he crossed the border.

He made good time heading out of Florida, but as it turned out, he really didn't need to. Marjorie's body wasn't discovered until several days later, when her rug-salesman husband Samuel came back around attempting to make amends.

Residents of Atlantic Beach were a close-knit community, and they all turned out for her funeral and interment in Warren Smith cemetery. Three villages on the coast of the Atlantic, united in mourning for a senseless death while her killer got away scot-free, roaring up the highway with the windows down and the autumn wind blowing in his hair.

An investigation into the murder of Marjorie Howie was undertaken by the local police, but their attempts to discover what had happened to her hit a dead end almost immediately. She had been seen in a local bar that night, but none of the witnesses could recall anything unusual happening, and everyone interviewed claimed that she was still there when they had departed. Even the bar staff couldn't recall whom she had been with over the course of the night, or whom she had left with. Even the time that she left the bar eluded the police, and they were forced to rely upon the vague window of the coroner's report to determine when she was likely to have been killed.

All of her neighbours in the block of apartments where she'd lived recalled nothing out of the ordinary that night. Not a single sound that wasn't entirely commonplace. No comings and goings at odd hours. Not even the raised voices that they'd often heard from the apartment during Marjorie's regular squabbles when her husband came to visit.

As a result of that particular bit of information, Samuel Howie remained the prime suspect in the investigation for many months to come until fresh evidence finally presented itself and most of that suspicion finally drifted away, though not before his reputation and relationships within the town had degenerated almost to the point that they were beyond saving. He'd lived in the Beaches for most of his adult life, and now he was like a stranger to these people all over again. The kind of man that they'd never be certain hadn't choked the life out of his wife. Even if the tide of public opinion turned eventually, he would have had to live the rest of his life knowing that all those people smiling his way from the roadside as he drove along had believed that awful lie about him.

Another life ruined, just because it made Paul's a little easier.

Killing Time

Practicality had been the name of the game for Paul up until this point. When he had killed, it had been out of necessity—so that his other crimes would not be discovered. He had focus and purpose for all of his actions, and the murder was done with that purpose in mind. After killing Marjorie Howe, selling her belongings and slipping through the police dragnet with ease, Paul lost that purpose.

Once more, he was in his basic state of being: he had money, he had a car, he had his freedom. Yet once more, he found nothing satisfying about it. Where before every day had been a joy, now he slipped deeper and deeper into ennui. Drink and drugs eased it, but he avoided excess now. He was still holding to his new philosophy of self-control.

The trouble was that he had always intended on rewarding himself for his restraint, balancing out the bad with the good, but as he drifted from town to town, heading north but otherwise aimless, he couldn't quite see any way that his new lifestyle was benefiting him. He needed to make it start rewarding him, or he knew that he was going to go back to his old ways, get sloppy, get caught.

That was when a hitchhiker appeared by the side of the road, up ahead.

He'd been known to pick up pretty young girls when he saw them by the side of the road in the past, flirting and chatting and winning them over. The kind of girls you found roaming out in the middle of nowhere tended not to be overly concerned with their reputations, and it worked out well for both of them. She'd get a ride, he'd get a ride, everybody was happy. Except today, Paul was not happy. He was bordering on depressed after so long without excitement, and he found that when his attempts at flirtation were rebuffed, he didn't find it quite so easy to shrug it off as a loss. This girl should have known her place. She should have known that there was a toll to pay for a free ride. It sparked off some anger in his gut, like he'd been cheated out of something he was due. Like he'd travelled across the country only to have the door slammed in his face by the woman who claimed that she loved him.

He drove off into the backroads, snapping, when the girl complained, that he was the driver and he knew the way. That only made her more suspicious and antagonistic. They argued as they went, Paul's anger now being fuelled instead of left to simmer down and as he pulled to the side of the road, fully expecting to just yell at her to get the hell out of his car and walk if she knew so much better than him. It was a surprise to him when he hit her instead. When he went on hitting her. Dragging her out of the car by her hair. Tearing her clothes off her as she struggled to get free, forcing her down into the dirt and mounting her, claiming her like he was entitled to do. And when she still went on fighting him, screaming in his face as he had his way with her, it was the best he'd ever had. It was exciting in a way that nothing before had ever managed to be. He was stronger than her, he was free, he could choose to do whatever he wanted with his life, and now he could do whatever he wanted with her. Her life was in his hands. Those hands locked around her throat as he was in the final throes, and when orgasm came, they clamped down, silencing her screaming, stilling her flailing arms. She bucked and writhed beneath him as she died, and he had never felt anything so good.

This was where his path had led him, to a place where he could kill when he pleased. And now, for the first time, he realised that it pleased him greatly. Killing felt good. Owning her felt good. Being the biggest and the strongest and the best, it all felt amazing. He felt like a god as the body still wrapped around him began to cool.

In keeping with his new philosophy, he was careful to properly hide the body when he was done, dragging her well clear of even these back roads and dumping her amidst the tangled kudzu that was swallowing up the wild places. With just his bare hands he'd taken her life and hidden her beneath those fast-spreading vines, to be swallowed back down into nature and never be seen again.

Her body would not be found for months, decay and scavengers having stripped her of all identity by then. To this day, her name and true identity still have not been found.

Buoyant after that experience, Paul continued up into the backwoods of Georgia with a fresh perspective. Since coming up with his new life plan, he had been neatly dividing business and pleasure, separating the part of him that killed from the part of him that lived. Now it had become apparent that there was no need for such partitioning. Not when there was so much joy to be found in every part of life, even the taking of it.

Drifting away from the major population centres where he suspected the police presence would be heavier, he found himself in Musella on August 23, when his money started to run low and his bloodlust started to run high.

Kathie Pierce was different from his previous victims in many ways. She was a young mother with a three-year-old son, chattering away by her side in her kitchen when she heard a knock at the door in the middle of the afternoon. It should have been a perfectly safe thing to go and answer it, something so commonplace in that quiet corner of America that she likely didn't even think about it, just dawdling through to pull open the door at the same time a stranger pulled open the screen door beyond it. At first, she took him for a travelling salesman. He had that same easy smile and charisma that so many of them cultivated. He wasn't as clean-cut as the majority of the door-knocking, encyclopaedia-selling lot, but she found that just added to his charm.

They exchanged greetings and pleasantries, and she could tell throughout it all that he was looking for an invitation inside. He hadn't even started with a sales pitch, hadn't even told her what it was he wanted from her, other than to come inside.

He had a toe in the door and that same slick smile locked in place when she told him that she was too busy right now. He had the same smile on his face when he pushed her back into the hallway and carefully shut the door behind him. He had the same smile when she loudly declared that if he didn't get out of her house, she was going to call the police.

Ready to call his bluff, she stormed through to the living room and picked up the telephone receiver, holding it up by her ear, fingers hovering over the rotary dial. One last chance for him to turn tail and run.

He closed the distance in a blink, smile never wavering. He snatched the phone from her hand and looped the coil around her throat. Just like he'd choked out Marjorie Howe, he was murdering this poor woman for no greater crime than existing.

She struggled, as it was in the nature of all living things to do in the face of their demise, clawing helplessly at his hands, at her own neck, at the cord of the phone. Blood ran from where she'd scratched into her own throat, but it did nothing to ease the pressure.

Her eyes bulged, her face darkened, and at some point in the proceedings, Paul's attention drifted from her to the little boy standing in the doorway, watching. He held the boy's gaze, fascinated by the way that he did nothing at all as his mother died. He went on watching him throughout, following the confusion mounting on the boy's face. Everything that was happening was so far beyond his realm of experience that he could not even grasp it, and in a strange way, the cruelty of that was more exciting to Paul than the killing itself. He was not killing one woman anymore—he was destroying this child's life, destroying his mind. He would haunt that little boy in every quiet moment from this day on. Raping and killing may have made him feel like a god, but in the eyes of this child, he would be the Devil. Forever. A living nightmare that would never end.

Paul had intended to have his way with this housewife, but looking into that little boy's expression as he struggled to comprehend death was somehow more appealing. Even after the mother was dead and limp, hanging from the cord-cum-garotte in his hands, he still held her there, watching the boy. Waiting to see what he was going to do next.

As it turned out, the answer was nothing at all. Eventually, even Paul became bored, dropping the dead woman and setting off to rob the house, moving from room to room, searching for valuables with one ear cocked, just waiting for the boy to scream, to cry, to run for help. He didn't. Even after Paul had cleared out the whole house, that child was still standing there, in the very same spot, paralysed by what he had just seen.

He stopped in front of the boy before he left, weighing his options. He could kill him, probably more easily than not, but he didn't really want to. He wanted the boy to live, to remember. He wanted to be all of the things that he had become in that brief moment that the kid had been staring at him. Taking his mother away. Leaving a witness behind ran contrary to his new plan, but this was just too delicious to destroy. He gave that boy one last look, to record this in his memory forever, and then he left him standing there in the desolation of what had been a home.

The police would arrive eventually, after his father came home and discovered what had happened. There would be an investigation, and the boy would be interrogated, over and over, in a desperate attempt to extract anything useful from amidst his trauma. Each time that he was questioned, he relived what he had seen. Each time, he slipped back into the same eerie silence. The police had been able to piece together the sequence of events from what little evidence was left behind, and the boy managed to corroborate some parts of that, but when it came to a description, he had nothing at all. The bad man had smiled at him, and that was all he could remember.

As for Paul, his wallet was full to bursting once more, and he was on the road again and long gone before anyone even knew he'd been there. In the days that followed, he crossed another state line, kept his head down, enjoyed himself as best he could in the bars he found while carefully ensuring that he never flashed too much money or drank so heavily that he might be tempted to misbehave. Killing the hitchhiker had felt good, but he'd put that down to the sex. Killing that woman while her little boy watched, he swore that had felt even better. The hitchhiker—she'd been a flash in the pan, a spark of joy to pull him up out of his depressive slump, but this was something that he was going to cherish. This was something he was going to remember until his dying day.

Smiling his crooked shark's grin, he polished off his beer and headed out to the car and the waiting road.

The warm memories kept him going for longer than he would have thought, and it was almost a week and a half later before he felt any inclination to rob or kill again. On the third of September, sitting in Scott's Inn, some roadside dive bar in Lima, Ohio, he began to move into the same routine he'd used on Marjorie Howe: identify a single wealthy female, isolate her before the night wound down, charm her, follow her home, do whatever felt natural after that. Except there didn't seem to be any handy wealthy widows lounging around just waiting for some bright-eyed young man to come and pick them up. Instead, he found himself sitting by the bar talking with a businessman named William Bates.

There was something of the salesman in Bates, and he seemed to recognise a kindred spirit in Paul, falling into the rhythm of rounds of drinks like they were old friends. Over the course of hours, they talked about near everything that they could think of, everything going on in the world, about work,—which his darling wife could never stand to hear a word about when he headed straight back home—and even about her and the rest of his extended family. Paul might not have been quite so forthcoming with details about himself, but it was clear that he was a man on the road, that he had an eye for the ladies, and those few anecdotes that he did contribute to the conversation were gems that William was probably going to pretend were his own next time he was away at a conference. The man could drink, and they spent more time laughing than William could rightly recall at any other point in the last decade or more. It almost made him sad that the guy was going to be gone come morning because it felt like he'd just fallen in with his oldest best friend.

All the more reason to make the most of the night. They went on drinking long after he should really have been heading home for dinner, but cold pot roast was a fair trade-off for this kind of fun. It was long dark by the time that the two of them staggered outside, arms slung over each other's shoulders, still laughing about some story that Paul had told involving some hitchhiking girl who didn't seem to get what she was trading for her ride to Florida.

Neither one of them should have been getting behind the wheel of a car, and they both knew it, but somehow the two of them poured into the front seats of Paul's with the promise of a ride home safe.

Turned out Paul did handle his liquor far better than William could have guessed. He pulled out of the parking lot without a scratch, practised and easy. The car was a weird fit for him, not the sort of thing you'd expect this kind of guy to drive, but William was too far gone to question why it looked more like it belonged to his grandmother than him. They fell back into their comfortable back and forth as they sped along through the night, and he didn't even notice the humping and bumping as they went from motorway to back road to dirt track.

On and on they went until, even through his inebriation, William came to realise that they'd been driving too long. He peered out at the trees passing them by and realised that somewhere along the way they had really taken a wrong turn. It was funny, they both laughed about it. About being lost and drunk and stupid. Except only one of them was all three of those things in truth, and one of them was laughing at the other's expense.

Eventually, even Paul had to admit that they needed to stop and get their bearings. William fumbled with the glove box, looking for a map, but all he found were leather gloves that would barely fit over Paul's thumb and a bus-tour brochure for someplace in the ass end of Florida. He laughed about it. Laughed about everything, the whole ridiculous situation. Paul stepped out of the car, strolled around, opened up the passenger's side and, like he was being chauffeured out here to the middle of the woods, William stepped out grinning.

With a lurching step, he closed the distance to Paul, who caught him before he could fall, and it was only after the fact that William noticed that he'd caught him around the neck. The laugh they'd been sharing went on, but it was only coming from Paul now. He laughed and he laughed as he squeezed tighter around William's neck, as he rode him down into the dirt and pine needles, as he choked the life out of him.

In a straight fight, maybe William could have defended himself, but blind drunk, choked and already pinned under the other man's weight, he was as close to helpless as any of the women Paul had preyed on until now. There was no real fear in him as he died, only confusion. Why was Paul doing this? What had he done? What had changed so suddenly?

When it was done, Paul retrieved the dead man's wallet and keys then dragged the body off deeper into the woods where it wouldn't be found so easily. Not that anybody was liable to come looking for him all the way out here anyway.

The only loose end was William's car, still parked outside of Scott's Inn, but it was a long time until dawn, and it was about time that he dumped the one he'd been driving since Florida anyway. He dumped his ride a little way down the road and then lugged his few belongings the mile up the road to the now silent bar to pick up his new wheels and head out on the open road once more.

William Bates was reported missing by his wife the following morning, but searches for him proved fruitless until late in October when his body was found.

As well as the car and cash, Paul now had all of William's credit cards, and he was not shy about using them. He was vaguely aware that his purchases could be tracked through them, so he mostly used them to take out cash, but he wasn't concerned about the information that was being recorded, not when it was leaving a trail of breadcrumbs suggesting that the dead man was alive and well, off on a bender, abandoning his wife and child — instead of rotting beneath a log in the woods.

It did not take long to max out all the cards, then he simply tossed them off the side of the road as he was rolling along the motorway. The end of a breadcrumb trail leading to absolutely nowhere.

As for Paul himself, he had no fear of the withdrawals being used to track him down. He had been swaying erratically north and south in his journey through Indiana, Kentucky, and Illinois, and now that he had no more reason to, he made excellent time heading out West.

His end goal was Sacramento, California, but that did not mean he was unwilling to take some detours and enjoy the road. Crossing down from Utah to Nevada, he pulled up into a rest stop near Ely on September 18. There was a campervan already there, an elderly couple going on a grand tour. Emmet and Lois

Johnson. He sauntered over to greet them and they had a good little conversation going before it all went sideways.

It was as though somebody had flicked a switch, and suddenly the nice young man who'd helped them set up their folding chairs in the shade of the Winnebago was in motion, hands locked around Emmet's throat. Now, Lois wasn't shocked to silence like some of the wilting flowers he'd gone after in the past. She had a lifetime of experience with the chaos of the world and how swiftly things could go awry. She screamed bloody murder from the moment the stranger laid hands on her husband, beating at his broad back helplessly, trying to pull him off. It was no use. Paul was relentless.

The chair broke under the combined weight of both men, and they went down into the dust. Emmet's face had turned purple, his eyes blood red where vessels were bursting. Try as she might, nothing Lois did could loosen the madman's grip on him. She clawed her way up the steel steps of the campervan, stumbling into the kitchen, raking through the cupboards and drawers for a knife, for a pan, for anything she could use as a weapon to save him. Finding a steak knife, she turned on her heel and found herself face to face with the killer.

Paul smiled at her—the same way he had when he first greeted them. All bright and charming and cheerful. Just another traveller on the highway of life.

His fist took her in the jaw, the other hand reaching down casually to twist her wrist until it snapped, knife falling uselessly to the sticky floor. It was ungodly hot inside the campervan in the Nevada sun. Everywhere that either one of them touched, sweat seemed to adhere them to. Her legs stuck to the edge of the fold-down table. Her back to the faux-wood panelling. His hands stuck in the wrinkled folds of skin beneath her chin, dragging and tearing at paper-thin skin, blood running down to join their sweat as she died.

He took whatever cash was ready to go, and left any valuables he couldn't stow in his pockets. He still had money enough to get him to Sacramento, so in truth there had been no desperate need for this crime. He was simply bored, and he saw an opportunity arising.

It was a little like his old crimes, when he'd act on the spur of the moment. He'd almost considered it a little treat for himself, to have a couple of little roadside murders, but what happened afterwards was as cold and calculated as anything he had ever done.

Forensics may not have been advanced in the 1970s, but there were certain things that Paul knew would tie him to this crime. Things that he proceeded to methodically eliminate. To cars passing by, the dead body outside was hidden. There was no more space to park at the rest stop, so he had no fear of discovery yet. He had all the time in the world to wipe his fingerprints off everything he'd touched, to clean himself up in their little cubby of a bathroom and to toss bleach around to ruin any other forensic evidence that he had not conceived of. His knowledge of science was limited, but he was more than capable of repeating the motions that he'd heard other prisoners talking about.

Most of the time, the trade-off wasn't in favour of this sort of scene cleaning. Most of the time, the extra time spent in the homes of his victims just increased the odds of him getting caught out—he'd learned that lesson hard in his burglary days—but there was a certain satisfaction to it that he just could not deny. Knowing that no matter what he did, it could never be tied back to him. Sure, he could cock up when he was selling things along, misjudge a fence or a pawn shop owner, but after all this time, he felt like he had a good sense for them. This meant that after he got into William's car and drove away, it was as if he had never been there at all.

For reasons that remain unknown, Paul then switched course again, perhaps realising that he was drifting back in the direction of the woman he had loved, and that being too close to her would only remind him of that anguish.

In just three days he'd made his way down to Texas, and as he was passing through Seguin, he spotted a female motorist who had broken down at the side of the road. Charlynn Hicks' car troubles offered him the perfect excuse to pull over and interact with her, even earning her trust when he acted as though he might be able to get her car running again. Dragging her by the hair, he hauled her down the slope by the side of the road and out of sight of any passing motorists before proceeding to rape and strangle her to death in exactly the same way that he had the hitchhiker only a few weeks before. The high of this killing was less than he had anticipated, even though he still enjoyed himself immensely, and it was only when he had finished with her that he realised that the killing was the part that had done the most for him. Not the rape. Unable to hide her body undercover as he had with most of his previous victims, he instead dragged her down to the barbed wire fence sectioning a ranch off from the public roadway and then proceeded to push her through, taking care to put her face into direct contact with the barbed steel at every opportunity. Mangling her and flaying away so much of her flesh that the face became unrecognisable to the degree that she could not be correctly identified even after the body was discovered.

As with most of his earlier discoveries about himself, it seems that it took Paul some time to become accustomed to the idea of himself as a thrill-killer rather than a rapist who was doing what was necessary to ensure he was never prosecuted, but by the time that he rolled into Birmingham on September 23, he seemed to be settled into this new version of himself. It had strayed far from his original vision of himself as a free-spirited rebel and into outright evil, but given the hand that life had repeatedly dealt him, he considered his new form to be only appropriate. A woman had hurt him, broken him down, ruined the joy and freedom that he had once considered to define him, so now he was hurting women and feeling some measure of justice intermingling with the simple joy of destruction.

In one of the less reputable bars of the city, Paul met a beautician by the name of Ann Dawson. She was everything that he had worked so hard to avoid being throughout his life. Someone stuck in a rut, trapped in a job she barely liked to pay rent on a place she didn't like at all. In her, he could see the same hunger for freedom that drove him, and in him, she saw a handsome stranger who was willing to take her away from her drab and dreary life to go and live an adventure at last.

Instead of inserting himself into her life and robbing her, he took her on the road with him instead. She footed the bills for the hotels they stayed in and the bars they drank in, and it seems that with the latest revelations about himself, Paul was able to perform in the bedroom without the need for any undue violence. They trolled back and forth across Texas for a while, sampling what hedonistic pleasures were available, Ann having the time of her life and Paul showing every sign of enjoying her company right up until the moment that he became bored with her.

On September 29, just six days after he had first picked her up, Paul murdered her and disposed of the body in such a way that it still has not been found. If not for the testimony of witnesses, it would have been as though the poor woman had disappeared from the face of the earth without a trace. He would later claim that he had thrown her into the Mississippi River, but for obvious reasons, this has never been confirmed.

This would become a new pattern of behaviour for him, similar to the brief dalliances he had conducted before his deep dive into depravity, where he would find an attractive older woman to finance him for stints, sharing in a brief honeymoon period of a romantic relationship until his interest turned stale and they were eliminated in exactly the same way as the rape victim one-night-stands.

For the following two weeks, Paul remained on the road, leaving behind scarcely a footprint on the surface of the earth. Drifting, he was spotted briefly in Oklahoma, Missouri, Iowa, and Minnesota, still living his same quiet life of bars and cars, avoiding attention where he could and keeping his lust for death under wraps until he'd put a good few states between him and his last victim.

By October 19, that restraint wore out. He needed to feel something again, something real. So, in the town of Woodford, Virginia, he set out to kill.

There was something almost clinical in the murder that followed. There were none of the usual alternate motives muddling the scene of the crime when it was discovered. No rape, no robbery, nothing but the killing itself. Even that was eerily clean. He forced his way into the home of 53-year-old Doris Hovey, found her husband's rifle, and killed her with a single shot before wiping it down carefully to remove his prints and laying it down on the ground beside her body.

Local police were baffled at this completely motiveless crime. Suspicion was invariably cast upon her husband, but his alibi of being at work was supported by literally dozens of witnesses. Not to mention the fact that he had been extremely happily married to her his entire adult life with neither one of them giving any indication to the contrary.

The job was so clean, it looked professional, and the local police resorted to investigating her for connections to organised crime that obviously were not there.

Despite the lack of up close and personal contact with Hovey, it seemed that Paul had found whatever release he was looking for through killing her. The simple act of killing itself was now giving him such joy that even doing it in such a cold and detached manner was sufficient to allow him all the satisfaction that he needed.

He continued drifting after that without any burning need to stop. Still guided by the landmarks of his past, he ended up heading back down towards Florida once more. Rationally, he probably could not explain the places that he was drawn towards, but in a way, it seemed almost like he was still a child pushing against the limitations and rules that had been set on him. Florida was the last place that he had known a serious crime might be connected to him, and on this account he had been carefully avoiding it, but now he wanted to see just how much he could get away with.

In Key West, he encountered a pair of hitchhikers, young women both, seeking a ride up to Miami, which he of course told them was his destination, too. All three of them clambered into the dead William Bates' car and headed away from the bright lights of civilisation and off into the backroads that Paul considered to be his domain. As much as he wanted to push his luck, he still had some good sense, making sure to keep the conversation pleasant and the journey feeling safe as he took them well away from the place where he had abducted them.

It was at this point that two mistakes happened, one on the part of Paul, and one on the part of the Florida State Police.

While heading along his beloved backroads, Paul rarely paid much attention to the speed limit. More often than not, he was basically alone on the road, and he was so familiar with the curves and corners that he knew exactly how fast he could safely take them. Combining this casual familiarity with a desire to impress the young women in the car, Paul was going well over the limit when a police car parked off the road spotted him speeding by.

When he saw the flashing lights in his rear-view mirror, Paul had to make a split-second decision. Step on the gas and use his superior knowledge of the road to make an escape or pull over and try to bluster his way through. Normally it would have been a toss-up to decide which was the more likely to get him out of danger, but this time he had his passengers to take into consideration— a pair of potential hostages that he could use to prevent his arrest if fast-talking proved itself to be insufficient.

He immediately pulled up at the roadside to wait for the patrol car.

Sweat beaded on his forehead as he watched the jovial officer slip out of his own car and amble over. There was ample opportunity then to start up the car, slam on the accelerator, and get out of Dodge, but he resisted that impulse. He was not going to be a creature of instinct, but one of rational thought, and he had already settled on his plan of how he was going to deal with this.

Winding down his window, he gave the cop his best sheepish smile and made no attempt to hide the fact he knew he'd been speeding. He apologised, promised that he wouldn't do it again, that he knew he'd been foolish. He even managed to flush with embarrassment as the girl in the back seat giggled at him. He calmed the raging little part of his mind by reminding himself that she'd pay for that later.

Confronted with a young man who had been showing off for some girls, and who now looked suitably chastened, the cop laughed it off and told him to be on his way, keeping his nose clean in the future.

Paul genuinely could not believe his luck. It was like winning the lottery. If the cop had run the plates on the car, or taken one look at his driving licence, then there was no question that he'd now be under arrest or fighting for his life, but instead, he had just gotten away with murder yet again.

Pulling out, he made sure to keep himself under the speed limit until the cop car was out of sight, and even afterwards, he started paying intense attention to the laws of the road, to the point that he earned more giggles from his passengers.

While he autopiloted his way through the conversation that had restarted the moment the police were out of sight, his brain lurched into action. What he wanted, more than anything else in the world, was to have these girls. To do whatever he wanted with them and leave their cooling corpses hidden in some dark corner of the world where he'd never have to think of them again, but the cop had seen them. He had seen Paul with them, and if their bodies turned up somewhere, even so incompetent a policeman could not fail to make the connection.

So, showing the restraint that he had forcibly trained himself to show, he kept up the façade of being a pleasant and flirtatious driver happily giving some hitchhikers a ride in the direction that he was headed, dropping them off in Miami as he had initially promised and parting ways on good terms, no matter how much he may have been internally seething.

That close brush with the law had put the fear of justice into him once more, and Florida, which had once seemed like home, now seemed to be a hostile and dangerous place. Confronted with the frightening reality that he would eventually be caught, Paul decided it was time to start making preparations for that day.

For the Record

There was nobody in the world that Paul trusted, but there were some people that he knew were bound by a code of ethics so tightly that they would not willingly choose to betray him. He did not understand the intricacies of the law, but he knew vaguely how lawyer-client confidentiality worked, and that he was inexplicably not only able, but encouraged, to speak freely with his during his last brush with the courts.

Knowing that Sheldon Yavitz had offices in Miami, Paul found himself a payphone and called, rather than just turning up someplace that the police might have had the good sense to connect to him. On the call, the same lawyer who'd gotten him out of jail to go and meet up with Angela Covic repeatedly entreated him to turn himself in to the police, that things would go so much easier for him if he would surrender himself, and there would be no risk of life and limb. That was before he heard the full extent of what Paul was confessing, however.

This was an opportunity for Paul, to both unburden himself of any lingering guilt and to brag about his incredible achievements in the field of murder and rape, but for understandable reasons, his poor lawyer was incapable of taking it all in. For him, it had just been a normal day at the office—he had no idea that he was going to be apprised of such grotesque horrors. He stopped Paul, mid-story, and explained to him that if he wanted representation when the time came, then he was going to need a proper record of everything that Paul had done up until that point. He checked if Paul had enough money to live on, then told him to write down a full confession, with as much detail as he could muster.

Even with the degree of trust that Paul was already giving the man, this put him on his heels a little. That confession, in his own words, would be enough to seal any conviction against him if he ended up back in court. Of course, his lawyer had no intention of sharing what he told him with the police, or even letting anyone know that it existed. Paul was his client, and everything discussed between them could be considered protected.

So it was that Paul found himself holed up in a cheap motel on the outskirts of Miami with a cooler full of beer and a tape recorder sitting on the bed in front of him. He had a pack of a dozen blank audiotapes to fill up, and if he was going to do this, he planned to do it right, sharing his whole story, start to finish, no lies, no tricks, nothing but the truth of who and what he was and how he came to be that way.

The recording lasted long into the night, but by the end of it, he was satisfied that he had recorded a detailed listing of every murder he had ever committed. There had been some lesser crimes sprinkled in like seasoning, but the meat and potatoes of the story had been, and always would be, death.

The next day, he arranged to meet up with Yavitz at a neutral location and hand over the recordings. The transfer was made—even though his lawyer seemed less than happy to see him in the flesh, wishing that the man had just mailed him the recordings instead of insisting upon a face-to-face encounter.

Paul would set off again, back on the road, back to doing all of the awful things that he so loved to do, and those recordings would remain there in Miami, in his lawyer's possession.

The story that those tapes told have mostly been lost. Nobody was ever allowed to hear them except for a grand jury and Sheldon Yavitz himself. The tapes themselves would later be destroyed in a flood that wiped out a considerable amount of stored evidence from multiple cases, ensuring that future generations would never know exactly what Paul had confessed to. However, it is possible from comments shared by jurors, Yavitz, and Paul himself to ascertain that the full confession that he delivered contained considerably more killings than have been officially credited to the man. Upwards of thirty.

In some cases, the police checked his dates and location and realised that he could not have been responsible for certain crimes. In others, there was no body to be found, and no person reported missing. Of the remaining cases, many of them could genuinely have been the work of Paul Knowles, but there was an equal possibility that he had simply learned of a murder through the papers and was seeking the additional fame that a higher body count might bring him. It was impossible to tell for certain which, if any, of the crimes that he claimed in those tapes were actually his.

Among those claims which were seemingly more credible was the account of the murder of Ima Jean Saunders in Georgia, a thirteen-year-old that Paul knew as "Alma." At the time, her body had not yet been discovered so no details of any murder had been released to be public. However, upon close scrutiny it was noticed that her disappearance and the date on which Paul claimed to have killed her did not match, with several months between them, leading to a great deal of incredulity about the likelihood that any of his confessions were real.

If we accept that he simply confused his dates, however, then it is entirely possible that he was responsible for that murder, along with a spate of others.

Given the dubious nature of Paul's confession, many members of the police force outrightly rejected his claims to several of the murders he professed to have committed, including those of Lillian and Mylette Anderson.

One crime that latter-day criminologists have conclusively linked Paul to, thanks to the confessions made in these tapes, was that of Karen and Dawn Wine of Marlborough, Connecticut. According to his confession, he had forced his way into the home of the mother and sixteen-year-old daughter, binding and raping both of them and then killing them, all in close proximity to the other.

This matched up perfectly with the crime scene that had been discovered there and the gruesome evidence that he had left in his wake. The one thing stolen from the Wine household adds just a little bit of extra credence to the idea that Paul was responsible. It was a tape recorder. The same kind used to make his confessions.

From the moment that those tapes were handed over to his lawyer, everything that Paul did becomes much more difficult to trace and verify. Despite the doubt that has been cast on them, and their loss before they could be properly documented and explored, they nonetheless provided a direct link between Paul and the crimes that he had committed—a link that evidence alone simply does not provide. Between his forensic countermeasures and the way that he disposed of the bodies of his victims, proving that he had anything to do with them at all is increasingly difficult from this point onwards.

For instance, Eddie Hillard and Debbie Griffin disappeared on the Second of November while hitchhiking near Macon. Hillard's body was found in some woods near to where they were last seen, but Griffin's still has not been found. Circumstantial evidence can place Paul in the area, and the abduction and murder certainly seem to be well inside his wheelhouse, but there is no way to be certain because he never confessed to the crime and no evidence was ever found that could link him to it.

Just four days later, in Milledgeville, Georgia, we pick up his trail again with some certainty. In another of the dive bars he so loved to frequent, Paul met up with a man named Carswell Carr, and after drinking together for some time, it became apparent to that man that Paul had nowhere to stay the night, having failed to make a reservation at the local bed and breakfast before arriving in town. As a good Samaritan, Carr invited Paul to stay the night in the spare room of his house, and Paul was more than happy to be invited into this well-to-do stranger's home.

Back at the house, Paul had expected some degree of grandeur and a wife waiting on Carr hand and foot, but instead, it was a relatively small place where the man lived alone, raising his fifteen-year-old daughter Amanda as a single parent. Ultimately, it made what he was planning to do easier, but it also robbed him of the rich pickings that he had been hoping for. With an almost casual ease, after being introduced to young Amanda, Paul wandered over to the knife block in the kitchen, drew the biggest one he could find and stabbed Carswell Carr to death, brutally and abruptly. The young girl screamed and panicked and wept, but through all of that, she did not run, which was all that might have saved her.

Leaving the knife buried in her father's corpse, he closed in on the teenager and latched his rough hands around the soft skin of her neck, bearing her down to the ground and squeezing as they went. Killing the father, that had been a necessity, but this, this was a pleasure.

She struggled weakly beneath his grip, sobbing and flailing and making all manner of disturbing sounds, but it did not take long at all for her to succumb to his strength. It was too swift for Paul's taste. She died too easily. He had wanted more from her. He felt like he'd been stopped halfway through the dance by a partner gone lame. Furiously, he ripped the clothes from her still body, yanking aside what he could, tearing through what he could not, until finally she was laid out beneath him on the floor, surrounded by the slow spreading puddle of her father's blood.

He tried to rape her then, tried to have his way with her corpse, but he found that he couldn't. The spirit was willing but the flesh seemed to wilt. This had happened to him the last time he had tried to take a willing partner, too. Violence and sex were now too intertwined for him to be able to enjoy either one without the other. If the woman beneath him wasn't fighting him, if he wasn't hurting her, then he could get no pleasure.

Stripping the house of any belongings of value, he headed back to the car as swiftly as possible, trying not to think too hard about what he had just done or, more concerningly, what he had just failed to do. He was still a man, he was still able to have sex when he wanted to. There was no need for him to think about what had happened back there. It was because the girl was dead, not because she wasn't struggling. There were plenty of good reasons that he couldn't get it up then and there. Nothing to worry about.

More than anything else that he had done that night, his unexpected bout of impotence plagued him. He felt now like he had something to prove.

Which led to the next encounter with Paul Knowles that we know with certainty happened.

Sandy Fawkes was a journalist from Britain, giving some consideration to working in America. She had a series of interviews lined up with some of the more impressive publications, and she figured that at worst she was getting herself a holiday from the familiar drudgery of home. She met up with Paul, going by the name Daryl Golden, in a hotel bar in Atlanta on November 8. It is from this encounter that we'd later learn so much about Paul Knowles, the way that he operated and the way that he spoke to others. He was obsessed with his own celebrity, complaining frequently that he should have been a movie star by now with his looks and talent. After learning that Fawkes was a writer, he insisted to her that she'd have to write a book about him someday. Sandy was less than convinced that the man had ever done anything interesting enough to even warrant a paragraph.

Yet for all of his little eccentricities, there could be no denying that he was a handsome man, showing the slightly older Fawkes a good deal of flattering attention, even waiting up in the hotel bar while she ran out to complete one of her interviews just so that they could spend some more time together. She told him right off the bat that she wasn't going to be taking him to bed with her, and the easy way that he accepted that and didn't argue was actually one of the big contributing factors to why at the end of the night, she did take him to bed with her.

The sex was not so much disappointing as it was non-existent. On that first night, Paul discovered that he could not perform at all, despite all of Fawkes' apparent beauty. She was left dissatisfied, and that probably would have been the end of their liaison entirely if not for the fact that when she mentioned she was going to be heading out of town, as an excuse to break away from him, he offered to drive her to her next interview.

Never one to turn down a free ride, Sandy made use of her on-call taxi service extensively in the days that followed, heading down into Florida for one interview before zooming back up the other way, getting to enjoy a little bit of the scenery while Paul talked about the local beauty spots. He seemed to have a real love for the state, for all of America, really. Not the cities, but the wild places in between, the landscapes and the road above all else.

Every night, they holed up in a hotel room and made another abortive attempt to make love, and every time, Paul entirely failed to perform when confronted with a willing partner. He was clearly becoming more and more upset and frustrated with each of these failed attempts, almost snapping at Sandy when she tried to console him. He did not want to hear that he had other great qualities, or that sex wasn't everything. It mattered to him markedly more than any other great qualities.

On November the 10th, Sandy broke off the relationship at last, having made as much use of him as she felt like she could before guilt kicked in. She explained to him extensively that it was nothing to do with their bedroom problems, and that they were just heading in different directions, but that didn't seem to do much to calm Paul. Still, for all of his obvious disappointment in the way that their relationship was coming to an end, he was nice enough and polite enough to offer one of Sandy's friends a ride the following day. She was the wife of another journalist, a woman named Susan Mackenzie. Sandy almost felt bad still using him as a taxi service after their pairing had come to such an unfortunate finish, but he was the one who had offered, so she could hardly turn around and tell him not to. Particularly when she was so intent on not causing a scene.

It would not be until the evening of the next day, after a full day of interviews and work during which she hadn't spared Paul a single thought, that he would be abruptly brought back to her attention again by the police knocking on her hotel room door.

At first, she was horrified, thinking something had happened to the man after they parted company, but what the police recounted to her was a story infinitely more disturbing. Paul had picked up Susan as he'd promised, but instead of taking her to her appointment, he had started driving them out of town. When she'd objected, he pulled out a gun and explained with the same chipper tone as always that she was going to have sex with him or he was going to kill her.

She was out of the door of the moving car before he'd even finished the sentence, running for her life and her dignity. Slamming the brakes on, Paul leapt out to pursue her, and likely would have gunned her down in the street if it wasn't for the sheer luck that a police patrol car just so happened to be rolling by at that very moment.

The patrolmen saw what was unfolding before them and leapt out of their vehicle, too, running to position themselves between the hunter and his prey. Paul brandished his sawed-off shotgun at them, making vague threats as he retreated towards his car. The officers made a split-second decision between abandoning Susan here in the middle of the road or giving chase and pursuing her abductor. They opted for the course of kindness. A decision that would cost several more lives before all was said and done.

Belting off down the freeway, Paul was in a mental spiral. He couldn't have sex, the police were right on his tail, they'd seen him chasing after one of his victims with a gun, everything was coming apart at the seams. Everything that he had worked so hard for was crumbling. All of his restraint and his planning and the blood on his hands, would all be for nothing if it ended like this. He drove as though he had the Devil at his heels ready to clap him in chains, and given the way that Paul thought of the law, that probably wasn't so far from the truth of it.

Close Up

Staying close to home in Florida, Paul made his way to West Palm Beach. The car he was in was hot now that the cops had seen him—he needed to switch it for something new.

Beverly Mabee provided exactly that opportunity. He invaded her home with the same mix of charm and bluster as had served him so well so far, with the intent to rob her and, in particular, to make off with the keys to her car. She was disabled by long-term illness, unlikely to put up any sort of a fight, and for some reason that rendered her safe from his attentions. Paul was in the midst of an internal crisis, still trying to understand why he was responding to things in the way that he was, and on this account, he had fallen back onto instinct to guide him while his mind was otherwise occupied. Instinct told him to leave her alone, to let her live even though she'd seen his face. Paul's instinct only wanted women if they struggled against him.

Barbara Mabee Abel, Beverly's sister, unfortunately filled that bill. He abducted her from the home that she shared with her sister, taking her hostage and forcing her into the car before driving away. While he told them that it was to ensure that Barbara didn't do anything stupid like calling the police, the truth became apparent fairly quickly. Once they were out of town, he pulled into a pitstop and climbed on top of her.

He would only rape her once, on that first night, but it was an experience that would scar her for the rest of her life. He confirmed in that cramped backseat that he could only perform sexually with an unwilling victim. Confirmed to himself that he was now only capable of receiving pleasure when it came at the cost of someone else's suffering. The mental turmoil that had marked the whole encounter seemed to come to an end then. He seemed to understand what was happening in a way that he did not before.

Surprising both of them, when they arrived in Fort Pierce, he actually set her free with the warning not to speak about what had happened or he'd come back for her. Obviously, she immediately went to the police, and the whole state was soon on high alert, searching for him.

On November 16, Highway Patrol Trooper Charles Campbell spotted the stolen car parked up outside of Perry, Florida, recognised its significance, and made a cautious approach. Paul was sitting in the driver's seat, head back on the rest, eyes closed. He was taking a mid-afternoon nap.

Taking no chances, the cop pulled the door open and grabbed hold of Paul before he even had a chance to wake up, dragging him out of the car, along with any weapons he might have hidden there, and onto the tarmac.

In times of crisis or confusion, when his new rational approach would not serve him, Paul's instincts ruled. His instinct when he was being manhandled by the police had not changed since the first time that he was arrested. By the time that he was up and out of the car, his hand had already snaked across to the cop's belt, and by the time the two of them were standing, Paul had the man's service revolver out and levelled at his head.

Campbell froze. Nothing in his training had prepared him for this. Nobody had even mentioned it as a possibility. He went from being the arresting officer to being a hostage so fast that he could have blinked and he would have missed it. Paul cuffed him and put him in the back of his own patrol car before going to his own stolen vehicle and retrieving those few belongings he called his own.

Clambering into the front seat of the police cruiser, he was grinning widely, cackling to himself a little. Stealing another cop car had been on his bucket list, and now that he was here, he couldn't contain his excitement. Throughout it all, Campbell was speaking in his best attempt at a soothing voice, telling Paul to stay calm and not to make any hasty decisions. Telling him that turning himself in was the only way that this could end. Paul laughed in his face at that, but that was about all the interaction the poor man got.

They headed off down the road, flying past the speed limit within a few seconds as Paul realised the law no longer applied to him in this car. In the back, Campbell kept on trying to end things peacefully, explaining that there was no way any cop was going to be taken in by him driving one of their cars. Stating plain as day that stealing this car was the worst mistake anybody could make. That same feral smile shone back at him in the rear-view. Paul knew. That was why he already had a plan to acquire another vehicle.

The moment that another car came into view on the empty expanse of motorway, Paul turned on the sirens and lights, zooming up until he was almost bumper to bumper with the poor driver and staying close enough to touch until they had pulled over to the side of the road.

James Meyer had just been driving home before he got caught. He hadn't been speeding, hadn't done anything wrong at all, so far as he could tell. Yet there was the cop car, with its lights flashing and siren blaring. He wondered if his brake light was out. If there was some petty misdemeanour he had accidentally committed without even realising it. He'd always believed that the innocent had no reason to fear the police, but the moment those lights came flashing behind him, his immediate response was fear and confusion as he tried to work out what he had done wrong.

It was only when he was staring down the barrel of Paul's borrowed pistol that he realised he'd done nothing at all, but that doing everything right wasn't enough to save him from fate.

With two hostages now in tow, Paul cuffed them both and dumped them into the backseat before heading north with all haste, crossing the border into Georgia before sundown. It was in Pulaski County, Georgia, that he realised their value as hostages was fundamentally limited and that they'd serve his purpose just as well tied up out here as they would in the backseat of his car, making him nervous. If the cops knew he had hostages, they'd know he had them stowed away somewhere. If they didn't know, then having these two in the back, just waiting to give him a kick at a vital moment, wouldn't make any difference.

With the cuffs, he attached the pair to a tree, back to back, and was about to head on back to the car when he realised that nobody was going to find them out here, certainly not before he got through the current situation. That meant that they were just as effective as a deterrent to killing him regardless of whether they were alive or not. Alive or dead, they still worked the same, so what was the point of leaving witnesses behind? He turned and fired a single shot into each of them from Campbell's service revolver. Both hit in the head, both were instantly lethal. Satisfied, he headed back to the car.

That momentary delay to drop them off proved to be an error in judgement on his part. Now that the police were actually mobilised, he no longer had the usual lead time on them that the element of surprise granted. They knew he was in Georgia, knew he was armed, probably even knew what car he was in. So it should have come as no surprise to him that there was a roadblock up ahead, where the cops were checking papers before letting anyone proceed.

With those police cars spread out across the road and armed officers milling around between them, it would have looked like an impassable blockade to almost anyone else, but Paul wasn't anyone else. He was the kind of man that could snatch a pistol from a cop's belt. The kind of man who could draw a knife in a bar fight without even knowing he had one. When he saw the blockade, he picked out the weakest point and he stepped on the gas.

Chaos exploded out from that point of contact. The cars he struck spun across the road, crushing one cop alive and knocking a half dozen others to the ground. The remainder opened fire on his car as it swerved its way along the road, doing substantial damage and ultimately resulting in it careening off into a ditch before it had made it a mile more.

Grabbing his weapons and cash, Paul abandoned the car and set off on foot. By this point, the police had identified him as the man that they were all out hunting for, and helicopters and dogs had been deployed alongside the officers on foot. Some of the officers from the roadblock caught up to him and opened fire but only succeeded in hitting him in the foot, while his own returned fire was enough to pin them down.

Paul's familiarity with the police and their procedures came in handy once again. He had quickly calculated the maximum distance that they would search for him, centred on the car, and now was high-tailing it to get beyond that limit as quickly as possible. Despite the swarms of officers on foot, the dogs, and even the helicopters, he made it unseen beyond the perimeter of their dragnet so quickly that it surprised even him. He was laughing as he ran, almost maniacal, unbelieving that after all that he'd already gotten away with, he was going to get away from this scot-free, too.

In the dead of the night, after almost a whole day of running and bleeding, he leapt a fence, landing beside some old brick buildings that looked disused, and wondered if he'd be better hunkering down there until the storm passed or if he should press on towards whatever civilisation this old pile of bricks was on the periphery of. He was just about to take his first steps off down the road when he heard the all too familiar sound of a shotgun being cocked.

Turning very slowly, he raised his hands.

It was not a policeman, or a member of any of the myriad law enforcement agencies that they had called upon for help. It was in fact a civilian, a Vietnam War veteran by the name of David Clark. He was a hospital maintenance worker who had been out working on the decommissioned structure when he'd caught wind of the foot chase on his radio. He held Paul there until the police arrived to arrest him. Finally.

Paul attempted to bluff and bluster his way through the arrest, but by this point, his reputation had caught up to him. Information about his history had been shared across state lines once he had been caught fleeing over them, and gradually a picture of the spree of murders that he had conducted began to be stitched together. This was aided and abetted by Paul's willingness to talk endlessly about himself and what he had done. He had no shame by the time that he was dragged into court—he was proud of himself. He described himself to the press as the most successful member of his family. The fame that he had always craved was now his for the taking.

Just as other serial killers were achieving fame, so too might he. In fact, with his film-star good looks and charisma, there was an expectation that he might outstrip them all. Even the name that the press gave to him in the aftermath of learning how he picked up his victims seemed to aggrandize him: The Casanova Killer. A ladies man.

He was jailed and brought before the court on multiple occasions for the multiple charges levelled against him. His lawyer did a frankly spectacular job of managing both the legal aspects of the case and the public relations nightmare that was unfolding around him. It was not the easiest thing to prove his client innocent when his client insisted on bragging about the murders that he had committed to every reporter who would listen. The only reporter who was notable in her absence was Sandy Fawkes, who had returned home to England in the intervening time. She booked a flight back to America as soon as she saw Paul's face on TV. She'd have to attest to his whereabouts during their time together and see if she couldn't pry more details of his story out of him. It wasn't every day that a book like this landed in your lap, and she was nothing if not a professional.

While she waited for her chance at another interview with him, Sheldon Yavitz took his opportunity to turn over the taped confessions that Paul had made into evidence. There was no way that Paul was going to get away with a not-guilty verdict on any of his crimes, but there was a small hope that he might avoid the death sentence if he came clean completely.

For his part, Paul never had any intention of letting them cage him. After all of the court proceedings were through on December 18 and he was headed to a longer-term high-security holding facility, he made the police an offer that they could not refuse.

Even after he had been arrested and wrung out by every interrogator that Georgia could muster, the location of the dead Officer Campbell's service pistol still had not been revealed. Paul had kept that last card tucked in tight against his chest so that, as he was being taken out of the jail by the courthouse and into the car by FBI Agent Ron Angel and Sheriff Earl Lee, he could offer it up with a flourish. If they drove him to Henry County, he'd point out to them where he'd dumped the gun.

While Angel was reluctant to divert from their original plan, Sheriff Lee knew how important it was to the local department to retrieve that firearm before it fell into the wrong hands. There was no greater embarrassment to the police than one of their own guns being used to commit a crime. On this account, they made the diversion.

As they rolled along the motorway, Paul's favourite place in all the world, he picked the handcuffs that were used to secure him with a paperclip. Then, oh so slowly, he edged forwards to take a hold of the sheriff's pistol in its holster.

Ron Angel spotted him in the act.

Paul tried to yank the pistol free, discharging it and causing the car to swerve wildly out of control, but Angel did not flinch. The moment that he saw the gun in Paul's hand, he unloaded three rounds into the man's chest. He would never see the inside of a jail cell. He would never suffer the loss of freedom that he so dreaded. Paul died on the spot.

Ironically, while Paul may have died in exactly the manner that he planned, his legacy has never quite followed in its footsteps. While he was a prolific murderer, having killed over thirty people if the tapes he recorded are to be believed, he never achieved the fame of his contemporaries, in no small part because he died before the media frenzy about him could really reach its height. All of the interviews and analysis that other serial killers underwent in captivity, he missed out on, and on this account, he has mostly fallen to the wayside. For all that he wanted to be a star, it seems likely that he would have traded that fame for his freedom and, ultimately, that was exactly what he did.

There have been arguments made by criminologists that Paul was not, in fact, a serial killer but should more accurately have been described as a spree killer, with so many of his crimes occurring in rapid succession. However, it seems quite apparent that he went through the many stages of development that most serial killers experience, just at a vastly accelerated rate, skipping over the slow and organised phase when most serial killers make the majority of their killings to enter what is sometimes referred to as the berserk, or meltdown, phase that usually only occurs when they are in danger of being caught and are trying to 'go out with a bang'.

Paul may have suffered in unusual circumstances in his youth, and he may have struggled with his impulse control due to pre-existing mental health issues, but there can be no denying that sadistic pleasure rapidly replaced practicality in terms of his motivation. He may have begun his campaign of terror as a common criminal only killing to survive, but by the end of his murderous rampage, he had no interest in allowing anyone to survive.

Not even himself.

DROP DEAD DANGEROUS

Want More?

Did you enjoy *Drop Dead Dangerous* and want some more True Crime?

YOUR FREE BOOK IS WAITING

From bestselling author Ryan Green

There is a man who is officially classed as **"Britain's most dangerous prisoner"**

The man's name is Robert Maudsley, and his crimes earned him the nickname **"Hannibal the Cannibal"**

This free book is an exploration of his story...

"Ryan brings the horrifying details to life. I can't wait to read more by this author!"

Get a free copy of **Robert Maudsley: Hannibal the Cannibal** when you sign up to join my Reader's Group.

www.ryangreenbooks.com/free-book

Every Review Helps

If you enjoyed the book and have a moment to spare, I would really appreciate a short review on Amazon. Your help in spreading the word is gratefully received and reviews make a huge difference to helping new readers find me. Without reviewers, us self-published authors would have a hard time!

Type in your link below to be taken straight to my book review page.

US	geni.us/dropUS
UK	geni.us/dropUK
Australia	geni.us/dropAUS
Canada	geni.us/dropCA

Thank you! I can't wait to read your thoughts.

About Ryan Green

Ryan Green is a true crime author who lives in Herefordshire, England with his wife, three children, and two dogs. Outside of writing and spending time with his family, Ryan enjoys walking, reading and windsurfing.

Ryan is fascinated with History, Psychology and True Crime. In 2015, he finally started researching and writing his own work and at the end of the year, he released his first book on Britain's most notorious serial killer, Harold Shipman.

He has since written several books on lesser-known subjects, and taken the unique approach of writing from the killer's perspective. He narrates some of the most chilling scenes you'll encounter in the True Crime genre.

You can sign up to Ryan's newsletter to receive a free book, updates, and the latest releases at:

WWW.RYANGREENBOOKS.COM

More Books by Ryan Green

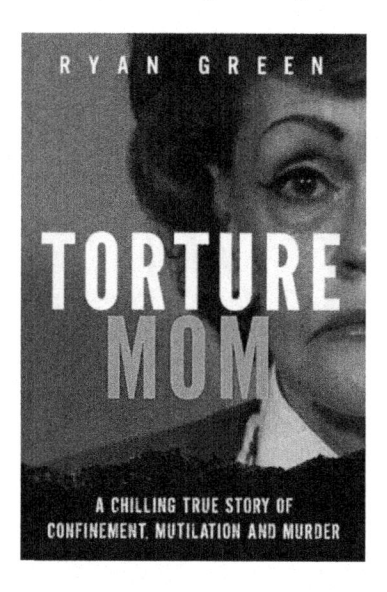

In July 1965, teenagers Sylvia and Jenny Likens were left in the temporary care of Gertrude Baniszewski, a middle-aged single mother and her seven children.

The Baniszewski household was overrun with children. There were few rules and ample freedom. Sadly, the environment created a dangerous hierarchy of social Darwinism where the strong preyed on the weak.

What transpired in the following three months was both riveting and chilling. The case shocked the entire nation and would later be described as "The single worst crime perpetuated against an individual in Indiana's history".

More Books by Ryan Green

On 29th February 2000, John Price took out a restraining order against his girlfriend, Katherine Knight. Later that day, he told his co-workers that she had stabbed him and if he were ever to go missing, it was because Knight had killed him.

The next day, Price didn't show up for work.

A co-worker was sent to check on him. They found a bloody handprint by the front door and they immediately contacted the police. The local police force was not prepared for the chilling scene they were about to encounter.

Price's body was found in a chair, legs crossed, with a bottle of lemonade under his arm. He'd been decapitated and skinned. The "skin-suit" was hanging from a meat hook in the living room and his head was found in the kitchen, in a pot of vegetables that was still warm. There were two plates on the dining table, each had the name of one of Price's children on it.

She was attempting to serve his body parts to his children.

More Books by Ryan Green

In 1902, at the age of 11, Carl Panzram broke into a neighbour's home and stole some apples, a pie, and a revolver. As a frequent troublemaker, the court decided to make an example of him and placed him into the care of the Minnesota State Reform School. During his two-year detention, Carl was repeatedly beaten, tortured, humiliated and raped by the school staff.

At 15-years old, Carl enlisted in the army by lying about his age but his career was short-lived. He was dishonourably discharged for stealing army supplies and was sent to military prison. The brutal prison system sculpted Carl into the man that he would remain for the rest of his life. He hated the whole of mankind and wanted revenge.

When Carl left prison in 1910, he set out to rob, burn, rape and kill as many people as he could, for as long as he could. His campaign of terror could finally begin and nothing could stand in his way.

More Books by Ryan Green

In 1861, the police of a rural French village tore their way into the woodside home of Martin Dumollard. Inside, they found chaos. Paths had been carved through mounds of bloodstained clothing, reaching as high as the ceiling in some places.

The officers assumed that the mysterious maid-robber had killed one woman but failed in his other attempts. Yet, it was becoming sickeningly clear that there was a vast gulf between the crimes they were aware of and the ones that had truly been committed.

Would Dumollard's wife expose his dark secret or was she inextricably linked to the atrocities? Whatever the circumstances, everyone was desperate to discover whether the bloody garments belonged to some of the 648 missing women.

Free True Crime Audiobook

Sign up to Audible and use your free credit to download this collection of twelve books. If you cancel within 30 days, there's no charge!

WWW.RYANGREENBOOKS.COM/FREE-AUDIOBOOK

"Ryan Green has produced another excellent book and belongs at the top with true crime writers such as M. William Phelps, Gregg Olsen and Ann Rule" –**B.S. Reid**

"Wow! Chilling, shocking and totally riveting! I'm not going to sleep well after listening to this but the narration was fantastic. Crazy story but highly recommend for any true crime lover!" –**Mandy**

"Torture Mom by Ryan Green left me pretty speechless. The fact that it's a true story is just...wow" –**JStep**

"Graphic, upsetting, but superbly read and written" –**Ray C**

WWW.RYANGREENBOOKS.COM/FREE-AUDIOBOOK

Printed in Dunstable, United Kingdom